THE MAGNET COMPANION

A Directory

A Complete and authoritative list of every Magnet published from 1908 to 1940, together with biographical information on editors and contributors and a comprehensive title index as an extra aid to the collector and researcher.

Also in this series:

THE DOWNFALL OF HARRY WHARTON
D'ARCY THE RUNAWAY
THE GREYFRIARS PRETENDER
THE BARRING OUT AT ST. FRANKS
THE GREYFRIARS HOLIDAY ANNUAL, 1928
THE MYSTERY OF WHARTON LODGE AND OTHER STORIES

THE

MAGNET COMPANION

A Collective biography, index
and directory

HOWARD BAKER PRESS, LONDON

THE MAGNET COMPANION
A Directory

First publication 1971

A HOWARD BAKER BOOK

SBN 7030 0006 3

Howard Baker books are published
by Howard Baker Press Ltd., at
The Greyfriars Press, 27a Arterberry Rd.,
Wimbledon, London, S.W.20

Printed in Great Britain by
DOUGLASS & GILSON MITCHAM SURREY

CONTENTS

ACKNOWLEDGMENT

The Publishers wish to record their indebtedness to Mr. W.O. Lofts for unstinting aid in the compilation of this book.

The World of

FRANK RICHARDS

The writing phenomenon known to the world as Frank Richards (real name Charles Harold St. John Hamilton) died at his home at Kingsgate, near Broadstairs in Kent on Christmas Eve, 1961. By that time it is estimated that he had written the equivalent of one thousand full-length novels. But although his stories had been loved for thirty years and more before the outbreak of the Second World War, it was not until the last twenty years of his life that he himself became well known and eventually had an entry in *Who's Who.* When he died there was a half column obituary in *The Times* and reports in all the other national newspapers. He had become a legend.

Born at Oak Street, Ealing, Middlesex on August 8th 1876, Charles Hamilton was the sixth in a family of five brothers and three sisters. His father, John Hamilton, was a master carpenter and one-time stationer, his grandfather a landscape gardener; and the family can be traced back to 1771, when a great-grandfather owned houses and The Black Horse Inn in Berkshire. Charles, who was a keen reader from an early age, was educated privately and also attended a Private School for Young Gentlemen – Thorne House School, in Ealing.

He wrote his first story in 1885. His early work is to be found mainly in The Trapps Holmes boys' papers and comics, and his output was prodigious. At one time he was writing at least six stories and serials every week, under about twenty different pen-names. Apart from school stories he wrote adventure, romance, travel, crime, humour and serious works.

In the autumn of 1906 he wrote his first stories of St. Jim's, in *Pluck,* and these were followed by the appearance in the new *Gem* in 1907 of Tom Merry & Co. In 1908 the best-loved and best-known school of all time – Greyfriars – appeared in *The Magnet,* detailing the adventures of Harry Wharton & Co. and – perhaps the most famous of all his characters, Billy Bunter, the Fat Owl of the Remove. *The Magnet* was to entrance generations of readers from 1908 to 1940.

In 1910 he created a new school in the Empire Library (featuring Gordon Gay & Co), whilst in 1915 the Rookwood stories of Jimmy Silver & Co. commenced in the *Boys' Friend,* later to be featured in the *Popular.* In 1919 he introduced yet another school – Cliff House – for the *Schoolfriend,* which was to delight millions of girl readers; although, to be factually accurate, he had introduced Cliff House in his Greyfriars stories many years previously. Whilst school stories were his favourite theme, he also created The Rio Kid, a Western outlaw, for the *Popular,* a South Seas Series, 'Ken King of the Islands' for *Modern Boy* and, for the same paper, Len Lex, the Schoolboy Detective; in addition to an unusual series called The School for Slackers. All this as well as his contribution to the yearly Holiday Annuals.

Frank Richards was a kindly, easy-going, impractical man who wrote because he enjoyed writing; the acquirement of money was a secondary consideration. He wrote with ease and as a consequence he was easily readable. As a further consequence, money came easily, and he spent it with equal ease, not bothering about the future but living only for the present.

In his stories he deplored gambling in any form; he made it quite clear that betting was 'a mug's game'. No keen reader of his narratives could have any illusions on that score. Yet Frank Richards himself appears to have been an inveterate gambler. When he was a young man his money went on the tables of the gaming houses on the Continent; later, the money he earned from his writing was carried away by slow horses. He put nothing by for the rainy day – in fact, it never occurred to him that there would be a rainy day.

World War II unhappily saw the end of *The Magnet* and, indeed, nearly all the juvenile papers. It seemed that Charles Hamilton's works were destined to disappear into obscurity, but with the publication of the Bunter Books by Charles Skilton and, subsequently by Cassells, the issuing of the Tom Merry Annuals and the B.B.C. television series featuring Greyfriars and the ubiquitious Bunter, not to mention Christmas plays at the Victoria Place, London, his characters suddenly acquired a fresh lease of life and brought Hamilton a deserved recognition and a renewed popularity.

Billy Bunter on television gained this plump character millions more admirers. After auditioning a very large number of artists, the B.B.C. found the perfect Bunter in actor Gerald Campion. Campion was a triumph in a role which many people thought could never be played successfully. Hamilton wrote the scripts for all the television plays, and Gerald Campion's acting added a new dimension to the character of the Owl of the Remove.

Hamilton's autobiography, published in 1952 and reprinted in 1962, was eagerly bought by his admirers and although it was in the main somewhat disappointing, it did reveal many interesting facts not only about the author but about his creations. At the height of his career he was writing a million and a half words a year, and they were written in Britain, Rome, Venice, Nice, Monte Carlo, Munich and other Continental cities. His foreign reminscences included descending into the crater of Vesuvius and hanging on to the outside of the Monte Carlo express!

It has been an almost impossible task to record all his work, but to date the compilers of his biography have discovered more than one hundred schools which he created, with a total of at least five thousand stories. So popular were they that well over three thousand were reprinted in various other publications. Almost 75% of the Schoolboys Own Library consisted of reprints of his works, and it is estimated that he penned a hundred million words during his lifetime.

In the last twelve years or so of his life, Hamilton turned again to one of the subjects which had dominated his own schooldays. Latin does not normally stand high on the list of a schoolboy's 'likes'; it is a stern and uncompromising language, and its literature is deficient in jokes.

Hamilton, however, had a love for Latin and a proficiency in the use of it. He also felt that the average schoolboy would have the same liking and proficiency if its literature could be made more attractive. After all, we had recently seen the publication of *Pinoculus* in Italy and *Winni-ille-Pu* in this country; why not *Bunteri Stultitia?* One instalment of it appeared in the Latin newspaper *Acta Diurna,* and others would no doubt have followed if Hamilton had lived longer. During 1961 he wrote a Bunter story in Latin which was published in *The Times Educational Supplement.*

His school stories were, however, always written in impeccable English, which is probably the reason why so many readers continued to absorb Greyfriars and St. Jim's long after boyhood was left far behind. Frequent references to classic literature were noteworthy factors in his school tales.

In his last years Charles Hamilton suffered not only from ill-health but from the greatest handicap that can befall a writer – failing eyesight. Despite this he never failed to answer the letters which continued to arrive from old and new readers, from all over the world.

On Christmas Eve 1961, the radio and TV gave the news of his death. Probably he received more coverage than any other writer of boys' fiction, and there were many who mourned the loss of 'Frank Richards', 'Martin Clifford' and 'Owen Conquest.' But although Hamilton himself had died, his brilliant character studies of boys and masters ensured his immortality.

Apart from the boys of Greyfriars – Harry Wharton and Co., Horace Coker, Vernon Smith the 'Bounder', Loder, Wingate, not to mention Billy Bunter, there was the unforgettable Mr Quelch, the Remove form-master, The Reverend Dr Locke, William Gosling, the school porter, Paul Pontifex Prout, and a host of others. All these, and many more, can be found within the pages of his books.

Without any question he had a profound influence for good on the youth of Britain during the first forty years of this century. He taught a splendid moral code, without the slightest suggestion of preaching or priggishness; a sensitive, gentle, scholarly man, who asked little and gave much. A character, too, in later years, with his black skull cap, his shawl, pipe and corduroy trousers with bicycle clips to keep out the draught. Withal a charming gentleman whose standards of moral decency and professional workmanship are regrettably conspicuous by being so unusual in the world in which he lived at the end.

Although the post-war years brought the return of Greyfriars stories in other formats, nothing quite recaptured the evergreen magic of the original paper until Howard Baker presented the first of his now world-renowned faithfull facsimiles. Each of these editions contains a complete series of stories from *The Magnet's* Golden Years. And each is a faithful fitting memorial to the glowing imagination, the humour and the humanity, the well-nigh incredible industry of its brilliant author.

'Frank Richards' loved writing for the young and affirmed that no writer could do any better work in life than this. Certainly none did it better than Frank Richards himself.

GREYFRIARS STORIES PUBLISHED IN THE MAGNET LIBRARY

No.	Date	Title	Notes
1.	15 - 2 - 1908	**The Making of Harry Wharton**	Arrival of Harry Wharton
2.		**The Taming of Harry**	Arrival of Herbert Trevor Arrival of Bob Cherry
3.		**The Mystery of Greyfriars**	
4.		**Chums of the Remove**	
5.		**Kidnapped**	Intro. Marjorie Hazeldine
6.		**Aliens at Greyfriars**	Arrival of Huree Singh
7.		**Rivals of the Remove**	
8.		**In Hiding**	Arrival of David Morgan
9.		**The Nabob's Diamond**	
10.		**The Captain's Election**	
11.		**Billy's Boom**	
12.		**Harry's Sacrifice**	
13.		**A Jolly Half Holiday**	
14.		**Billy's Competition**	
15.		**Wharton's Operatic Company**	Arrival of Micky Desmond
16.		**Stage Struck**	
17.		**A Jolly Outing**	
18.		**Roughing It**	Introd. Ernest Levison
19.		**The Greyfriars Challenge**	
20.		**Billy's Treat**	
21.		**The Famous Four**	Featuring Ernest Levison
22.		**Fun by the Sea**	
23.		**The Greyfriars Riot**	
24.		**Four on the Warpath**	Mr Chesham, the Faddist Form-master Series

25.		**The Triumph of the Remove**	
26.		**The Greyfriars Sleepwalker**	
27.		**The Reformation of Greyfriars**	Herbert P. Randall – Old Boy
28.		**The Remove Master's Substitute**	
29.		**The Greyfriars Conjuror**	Featuring Ernest Levison
30.		**Billy Bunter, Hypnotist**	
31.		**Harry Wharton's Task**	
32.		**The Greyfriars Ventriloquist**	Arrival of Robert Smith Minor
33.		**Aliens Against Greyfriars**	
34.		**The Rival Schools**	
35.		**Harry Wharton's Scheme**	Arrival of William Stott
36.		**The New Boy at Greyfriars**	Arrival of Wun Lung
37.		**They Greyfriars Chinee**	
38.		**The Cheerful Chinee**	
39.		**Greyfriars versus St Jim's**	
40.		**Billy Bunter's Raid**	
41.		**The Rival Entertainers**	
42.		**Harry Wharton's Day Out**	
43.		**The Greyfriars Victory (Double No)**	Featuring Ernest Levison Arrival of Donald Ogilvy
44.		**The Amateur Cooks**	Arrival of Donald Ogilvy
45.		**A Lad from Lancashire**	Arrival of Mark Linley & Sidney James Snoop
46.		**Expelled!**	Levison's Expulsion
47.	**2 - 1 - 1909**	**Home for the Holidays**	
48.		**The New Firm at Greyfriars**	Harry Wharton Saves Molly Locke
49.		**The New Sixthformer**	Arrival of Ionides
50.		**Harry Wharton's Campaign**	Molly Locke, Suffragette
51.		**Bunter's Vengeance**	

52.	**The Hero of Greyfriars**	
53.	**The Greyfriars Sailors**	
54.	**Billy Bunter's Housewarming**	
55.	**The Chinese Captain**	
56.	**Harry Wharton's Recruits**	
57.	**The Ventriloquist's Pupils**	
58.	**Cut by the Form**	
59.	**The School Dance**	Ionides at Cliff House
60.	**The Greyfriars Cricketers**	Cliff House versus Greyfriars
61.	**The Rivals of Greyfriars**	
62.	**The Shipwrecked Schoolboys**	
63.	**The Greyfriars Picnic**	
64.	**Wharton & Co versus Merry & Co**	
65.	**Rival Scouts**	
66.	**Stony Broke**	First mention of Loder, **not** a prefect
67.	**Harry Wharton's Ward**	
68.	**The Invasion of Greyfriars**	Cliff House School Stays at Greyfriars. 68-70.
69.	**The Bully of Greyfriars**	
70.	**The Cliff House Party**	
71.	**The Barring of Bulstrode**	
72.	**The Greyfriars Photographer**	
73.	**The Greyfriars Caravan**	
74.	**The Greyfriars Camp**	'Saucy Susan' Caravan Series
75.	**The Tenants of Study 13**	
76.	**Billy Bunter – Editor**	
77.	**The Greyfriars Bunfight**	
78.	**Harry Wharton's Bank Holiday**	D'Arcy & Minor in London

No.	Date	Title	Notes
133.		The Postal Order Conspiracy	
134.		Todd the Terrible	
135.		Captain Bob Cherry	
136.		Billy Bunter's Kickoff	
137.		Only Alonzo	
138.		Harry Wharton's 'Pro.'	
139.		Alonzo's Little Game.	
140.		The Cliff House Guest	
141.		The New Firm	
142.		The Duffer's Downfall	
143.		The Head of Study 14	First mention of Coker in the Shell
144.		Billy Bunter's Minor	Arrival of Sammy Bunter
145.		Coker's Catch	Coker Goes up to the Fifth
146.		The Leader of the New School	
147.		The Schoolboy Traitor	
148.		Bunter's Bust-up	Double Christmas Number
149.		The Haunted Island	
150.		The Yankee Schoolboy	Arrival of Fisher T. Fish
151.		The Girls' School Challenge	Arrival of Johnny Bull
152.	7 - 1 - 1911	John Bull Junior	
153.		Forward Fish!	
154.		Rolling in Money	Johnny Bull's Concertina is smashed
155.		Spoofing Alonzo	
156.		The Tempter	
157.		The Greyfriars Hypnotist	
158.		John Bull Jnr's Weekly	Early 'Greyfriars Herald' Series
159.		The Rival Weekly	

160.	**Poor Old Bunter!**	
161.	**Alonzo the Footballer**	
162.	**Wingate's Chum**	Doctor Locke finds his long-lost daughter, Rosie
163.	**The Artful Dodger**	
164.	**The Greyfriars Clown**	
165.	**The New Page**	Arthur Jolly, new boy – practical joker ss *H.C. Hook*
166	**The Greyfriars Wheelers**	
167.	**The Prisoner of the Priory**	Rosie Locke, prisoner
168.	**Last Man In**	
169.	**The Bully's Remorse**	Uncle Benjamin at Greyfriars
170.	**Harry Wharton's Downfall**	Bulstrode, Captain
171.	**The Greyfriars Tyrant**	
172.	**The School on Strike**	Mr Lathrop
173.	**Driven from School**	New Boy Heath
174.	**A Schoolboy's Honour**	
175.	**The King's Guest**	Wharton saves a Central European Prince from drowning and is received by the King at Buckingham Palace
176.	**Bulstrode on the Warpath**	
177.	**Barred by His People**	
178.	**The Bully's Brother**	Bulstrode's Brother dies in fire and Wharton Captain of Form again.
179.	**Bob Cherry in Search of his Father**	
180.	**A Schoolboy's Crossroads**	The Bounder Expelled
181.	**Saved from Disgrace**	The Bounder Returns
182.	**The Cock of the Walk**	Arrival of Bolsover

No.	Date	Title	Notes
183.		Inky Minor	Dicky Nugent Expelled
184.		The Schoolboy Millionaire	Arrival of Mauleverer
185.		The Slacker	Featuring Arthur Carlton
186.		The Only Way	Rupert Valance
187.		Driven to the Wall	Dick Russell in Limelight
188.		Ashamed of his Father	Cecil Leigh
189.		Sent to Coventry	Arrival of Mr Lang to take Mr Quelch's place
190.		The Outlaws of the School	
191.		An Ungrateful Son	
192.		Football Foes	
193.		A Schoolboy's Sacrifice	
194.		By Sheer Grit	Arrival of Penfold
195.		The Bully's Chance	
196.		For the Honour of his Chum	Skinner Expelled
197.		His Last Match	
198.		The Stolen Cup	Ferney of the Remove
199.		The Downfall of the Fifth	
200.		Wingate's Folly	Christmas Double No. Wingate in Love
201.		The Duffer's Return	
202.		Against His Father's Wish	Arthur Talbot of the Fifth, leaves
203.		By Order of the Form	
204	6 - 1 - 1912	The Parting of the Ways	Sidney Clavering leaves
205.		The Duffer's Double	First Mention of Peter Todd
206.		Bolsover's Brother	Bolsover Minor rescued from Slums
207.		The Schoolboy Moneymaker	
208.		Tempted but True	
209.		The Schoolboy Minstrels	

210.	**Bolsover Minor's Last Sacrifice**	
211.	**A Race Against Time**	
212.	**The Rivals' Test**	
213.	**The Jape against the Fifth**	
214.	**A Fight for the Captaincy**	
215.	**The Rival Co's of Greyfriars**	
216.	**The Schoolboy Outcast**	Arrival of Monty Newland
217.	**Schoolboys' Treasure**	Felice Cesare
218.	**Harry Wharton & Co's Windfall**	The Co. at Naples
219.	**A Forbidden Chum**	
220.	**Foes of the Fourth**	The 'Moocher'
221.	**Honour before All**	Vallence Expelled
222.	**A Traitor in the School**	Mr Roper, New Master (The 'Moocher')
223.	**Frank Nugent's Great Wheeze**	
224.	**The Road to Ruin**	Vallence returns
225.	**Out of Bounds**	Mr Harding of Trevelyan
226.	**Down on His Luck**	
227.	**The Greyfriars Gardeners**	
228.	**Bolsover Minor's Bolt**	
229.	**The Remove Form's Feud**	
230.	**The Schoolboy Detective**	Dalton Hawke, the schoolboy 'tec
231.	**The Stolen Schoolboys**	
232.	**The Circus Schoolboy**	Arrival of Arthur Banthorpe
233.	**Under Suspicion**	Gadsby of the Shell Expelled
234.	**Harry Wharton & Co's Bank Holiday**	The Co. in Blackpool
235.	**Spoofing the School**	
236.	**The Kidnapped School**	

No.	Date	Title	Notes	
237.		The Competition Craze at Greyfriars		
238.		The Formmaster's Secret	Dalton Hawke and Percy Punter	
239.		The Hidden Horror		
240.		The Tuck Shop Raiders		
241.		Coker Minor – Sixth Former	Arrival of Reginald Coker	
242.		The Greyfriars Insurance Company		
243.		The Schoolboy Sleepwalker		
244.		The Schoolboy Policeman		
245.		For His Mother's Sake	Mr Nugent leaves Mrs Nugent	
246.		The Terror of Greyfriars	Arrival of Theophilus Flipps, Faddist	
247.		Top Dog	Vernon Smith's Feud against the Famous Five	
248.		The Bounder's Triumph		
249.		The Greyfriars Crusaders		
250.		Sacked from the School		
251.		The Schoolboy Renegade		
252.		Mark Linley's Last Fight		
253.		Drummed out of Greyfriars		
254.		Bob Cherry's Barring-Out		
255.		Harry Wharton's Win		
256.	4 - 1 - 1913	The Greyfriars Pantomime		*ss Edwy S. Brooks*
257.		Fish's Fag Agency		
258.		Rake of the Remove	Arrival of Rake	
259.		Left in the Lurch		*ss Edwy S. Brooks*
260.		Harry Wharton & Co's Rescue	Bermondsley Babe, tramp	*ss Edwy S. Brooks*
261		Scorned by Greyfriars	Arrival of new boy (Tom Flynn)	
262.		A Split in the Sixth	Wingate resigns the captaincy	
263.		Captain Coker		

264.	A Son of the Sea	New boy 'Irish' Con Fitzpatrick
265.	The Captain's Minor	Arrival of Wingate Minor
266.	Bob Cherry's Secret	Bob's cousin, Paul Tyrell, as Games Coach
267.	Chums Afloat	Captain Curll
268.	The Schoolboy Conjuror	Arrival of Kipps
269.	Barred by the Fags	Jack Wingate in Coventry
270.	Bob Cherry's Chase	Paul Tyrell Again
271.	The Impossible Four	Arrival of Peter Todd
272.	The Schoolboy Moneylender	
273.	'Friars versus Saints	
274.	Standing by Skinner	Skinner returns
275.	Peter Todd's Chance	
276.	Wun Lung's Secret	Wun Lung takes opium
277.	Holding the Fort	Mr Snooks
278.	In Direst Peril	
279.	His Own Betrayer	New boy Frank Cleveland
280.	The Schoolboy Dramatists	
281.	Quits!	
282.	In Another's Name	Jem Gadd, blackmailer
283.	The Sandow Girl of Greyfriars	Johnny Bull's cousin, 'Fluffy'.
284.	Uncle Fish	
285.	The False Form master	Ulick Ferrers, second cousin of Mr Quelch
286.	The Sports of the School	
287.	Self Denial Week at Greyfriars	
288.	Shunned by the Form	Summer Double Number
289.	The Nut of Greyfriars	Arthur Brandreth, new boy
290.	The Schoolboy Shopkeepers	

291.		**Up Against It**	Mr Nutt, new Remove master	
292.		**Bunter the Prizewinner**		
293.		**The Moonlight Footballers**	Aunt Judy and Reggie Coker	
294.		**Bravo the Bounder!**		
295.		**The Sneak's Revenge**	Herr Gans featured	
296.		**The Greyfriars Herald**		
297.		**Game to the Last**	Vernon Smith breaking bounds to St Jim's	
298.		**The Vanished Schoolboy**		
299.		**The Greyfriars Golddiggers**		
300.		**The Coker Cup**		
301.		**Cast Up by the Sea**	Clive Cholmondeley	
302.		**The Biter Bit**		
303.		**The Scapegoat**	Hazeldine in trouble	
304.		**In Borrowed Plumes**	Gaston Duval, kidnapper	
305.		**The Four Heroes**	Double Christmas number	
306.		**Harry Wharton's Christmas Number**		
307.		**Good Old Coker**	Reggie Coker	
308.	3 - 1 - 1914	**Ructions in the Remove**	Herr Gans	
309.		**Held Up**	Captain Markoff	
310.		**The Right Sort**	Algernon Darell, new boy	
311.		**Trouble with Highcliffe**	Featuring Mr Mobbs	
312.		**Bunter's Black Chum**	Diniwayo, black footballer	
313.		**The Factory Rebels**	Mr Hardinge	*ss E.S. Brooks*
314.		**Peter Todd's Plot**		
315.		**The Snob's Lesson**	Sidney James Snoop	
316.		**The White Feather**	Arrival of Percy Esmond	
317.		**Blundell's Prize**		*ss E.S. Brooks*

318.	The Missing Chinee		
319.	Alonzo's Marvellous Mixture		
320.	Easy Terms		
321.	April Fools All		*ss E.S. Brooks*
322.	Wibley's Wheeze	Arrival of Wibley	
323.	The Runaway		
324.	Harry Wharton's Diplomacy	Arrival of Larry Lascelles	
325.	Coker's Plot		
326.	The Uninvited Guests		
327.	Rough on Coker		
328	Cornered	Fisher T. Fish	
329.	The Boy from the Farm	Arrival of Sir Harry Beauclere and his explusion	
330.	The Wrong Sort		
331.	The Missing Master	Featuring Mr Lascelles	
332.	The Greyfriars Trippers		
333.	The Dark Horse	Featuring Wally Bunter	
334.	The Shadow of the Past	Jerry Hawke	
335.	Looking After Uncle	The Todds' Uncle Benjamin	
336.	Wun Lung's Wheeze		
337.	My Lord Fish		
338.	The Match with St Jim's		
339.	Self-Condemned	Dicky Nugent and Ponsonby	
340.	Harry Wharton & Co's Holiday	Summer Double number	
341.	Wild Women at Greyfriars	Miss Boxer, Suffragette	
342.	Coker's Conquest	Coker's cousin Amy	
343.	A Cool Card	Arrival of Squiff	
344.	Ructions at Highcliffe	Cecil Ponsonby	

No.	Date	Title	Notes	Author
345.		**Spirited Away**	Arrival of Bertie Sylvester	
346.		**Hard Up**	Squiff's revenge on Ponsonby	
347.		**Changed by Adversity**		*ss E.S. Brooks*
348.		**The Greyfriars Spy-Hunters**	Herr Gans	
349.		**Won by Pluck**		*ss A.M. Kemp*
350.		**Foiling the Foe**	Dick Trumper	
351.		**The Photo Prize**		*ss A.M. Kemp*
352.		**Looking for Alonzo**		
353.		**The Reign of Terror**		*ss G.R. Samways*
354.		**The Black Footballers**		
355.		**Fagging for Coker**		
356.		**The Snob of the Remove**	Franz von Limburg, new boy	
357.		**The Return of the Prodigal**	Christmas double number	
358.		**Billy Bunter's Uncle**	Captain Bunter	
359.		**The Patriotic Schoolmaster**	Mr Lascelles	
360.	2 - 1 - 1915	**Skinner's Scheme**	Ferrers Locke at Greyfriars	
361.		**The Rival Ventriloquist**		*ss G.R. Samways*
362.		**The Fight for the Cup**		
363.		**The Cruise of the Famous Five**		
364.		**Surprising the School**	Featuring Cora Quelch	
365.		**The Schoolboy Auctioneer**	Fisher T. Fish	
366.		**Bunter the Blade**		
367.		**The Last Plunge**	Johnny Bull and Falke series	
368.		**Captured at Last**	J. Bull leaves for Australia	
369.		**Tom Dutton's Triumph**		
370.		**Through Fire and Flame**		
371.		**Bunter's Bank Notes**		

No.	Title	Notes	Author
372.	**The Hun Hunters**		
373.	**Carried Away**		
374.	**The Fall of the Fifth**	Double number. Featuring Ponsonby	
375.	**Special Constable Coker**		
376.	**When Johnny Comes Marching Home**	Return of Johnny Bull	
377.	**The Mystic Circle**	Mr Lucas Judd and Loder	*ss E.S. Brooks*
378.	**The Schoolboy Acrobats**	Arrival of Charles Chumgum	
379.	**Hurree Singh's Peril**	Ram Dass	
380.	**Heroes of Highcliffe**		
381.	**The Punishment Policies**		
382.	**The Slacker's Eleven**		
383.	**Fifty Pounds Reward**		
384.	**The Scout's Victory**		
385.	**The Old Boys' Challenge**		*ss G.R. Samways*
386.	**Mauly's Flirtation**	Miss Bella Bunbury	
387.	**The Schoolboy Lawyer**		
388.	**The Mystery of the Gables**	Mr 'Roff'	*ss E.S. Brooks*
389.	**The Mysterious Mr Mobbs**		
390.	**Sportsmen All**		*ss G.R. Samways*
391.	**The Master Who Stayed at Home**	Mr Lascelles leaves for the army	
392.	**Schoolboys Never Shall be Slaves**	Double Summer number	
393.	**Ponsonby's Plot**		
394.	**The Fellow Who Won**		*ss G.R. Samways*
395.	**At War With Greyfriars**	Mr. Bunn, new porter	
396.	**Backing up Bunter**	LAST RED MAGNET	
397.	**Coker's Canadian Cousin**		
398.	**A Lancashire Lad's Luck**		

399.		**Champion of the Oppressed**		
400.		**The Sunday Crusaders**		*ss G.R. Samways*
401.		**Bunter's Anti-Tuck Campaign**		
402.		**The Midnight Marauders**		
403.		**Straight as a Die**	Cecil Snaith expelled. New Boy Paul Sydney	
404.		**Going the Pace**		
405.		**The Remove Eleven on Tour**		*ss G.R. Samways*
406.		**The Conjurer's Capture**	Frederick Falke returns	
407.		**The Jape of the Season**	Mr Quelch in Search for Wife jape	
408.		**The Rebels of the Remove**	Rake in the Limelight	
409.		**Harry Wharton & Co's Pantomime**	Double Christmas Number	
410.		**Bunter the Masher**	Majorie Hazeldine	
411.		**The Bounder's Relapse**		*ss E.S. Brooks*
412.	1 - 1 - 1916	**Hazeldine's Honour**		
413.		**The Schoolboy Speculator**		
414.		**Bob Cherry's Challenge**		*ss G.R. Samways*
415.		**The Colonel's Cup**	The Colonel's Cup Series	
416.		**Fought For and Won**		
417.		**Foes of the Sixth**		*ss G.R. Samways*
418.		**Shielding a Scapegrace**	Cecil Snaith Returns	
419.		**Coker's Engagement**		
420.		**Flooring Fishy**		
421.		**Skinner the Skipper**		*ss G.R. Samways*
422.		**His Highness**	Rattenstein series	
423.		**When Friends Fall Out**		
424.		**The Mailed Fist at Greyfriars**	Sergeant Burrell	*ss G.R. Samways*
425.		**Micky Desmond's Luck**		

426.	**The Terrible Two**	Bob and 'Curly' Williams	*ss G.R. Samways*
427.	**False Evidence**		*ss E.S. Brooks*
428.	**The Upper Hand**	Mr. Black	
429.	**Coker's Conscript**		
430.	**The Forbidden Match**		*ss G.R. Samways*
431.	**The Hero of Greyfriars**	Bob Cherry saves Hilton Popper's niece	
432.	**The Boy from South Africa**	Arrival of Piet Delarey	*ss J.N. Pentelow*
433.	**Kicked out of School**	Rattenstein expelled	
434.	**Frank Nugent's Folly**		
435.	**Fighting to the Finish**		
436.	**Called to the Colours**		*ss G.R. Samways*
437.	**Run to Earth**		
438.	**Monsieur Wibley**		
439.	**The Other Bunter**	Reappearance of Wally Bunter	
440.	**The Giant of Greyfriars**	Mr Ransome, Games Master	*ss G.R. Samways*
441.	**The Schoolboy Farmers**		
442.	**Sticking to His Guns**	Slippery Sam	
443.	**His Own Fault**		
444.	**The Trickster Tricked**		
445.	**Rake's Rival**	Arthur Carthew	*partly written by J.N. Pentelow*
446.	**A Split in the Study**		
447.	**The Sentence of the School**		
448.	**The Great Bat Mystery**	Mr Braxton	*ss E.S. Brooks*
449.	**Billy Bunter's Bolt**		*ss G.R. Samways*
450.	**For D'Arcy's Sake**	Captain Punter	
451.	**The Mystery of Mauly**	Aubrey Spencer	*ss G. R. Samways*
452.	**The Stolen Study**		

No.	Date	Title	Notes	
453.		The Bounder's Guest		
454.		Fishy's Latest		*ss R.S. Kirkham*
455.		Under Bunter's Thumb		
456.		The Rascal of the Remove	Herr Gans featured	
457.		Mauleverer's Detective		
458.		Coker's Spy		
459.		The Rivals of Greyfriars		
460.		Billy Bunter's Reformation	Featuring Cora Quelch	
461.		The House on the Heath	Double Christmas Number	
462.		The Way of the Transgressor		
463.		Foul Play		
464.		Victims and Victors		*ss J.N. Pentelow*
465.	6 - 1 - 1917	Getting Rich Quick		
466.		In Hot Water		*ss J.N. Pentelow*
467.		The Deserter	Paul Tyrell	
468.		Linley Minor	Gerald Linley of the III	*ss J.N. Pentelow*
469.		Bunter's Big Brother		
470.		The Fellow Who Funked		
471.		Sir Jimmy of Greyfriars	Arrival of Sir Jimmy Vivian	
472.		The Great Fat Sure	Engensen	*ss Reginald Kirkham*
473.		The Herlock Sholmes of Greyfriars		
474.		Viscount Bunter		
475.		The Prefects' Plot		
476.		The Greyfriars Flying Corps		*ss G.R. Samways*
477.		Harry Wharton's Rivals		*ss J.N. Pentelow*
478.		The Rebel		*ss J.N. Pentelow*
479.		Colonial Chums		*ss J.N. Pentelow*

480.	The Remove Election Campaign		*ss J.N. Pentelow*
481.	Head of the Poll		*ss J.N. Pentelow*
482.	National Service at Greyfriars		
483.	Sir Jimmy's Secret		
484.	His Father's Honour	Bernard B. Tracy	*ss G.R. Samways*
485.	Two of the Sixth		
486.	Peter Todd's Vengeance		*ss J.N. Pentelow*
487.	The Fall of the Bounder	Fall of The Bounder series	
488.	The Bounder's Match		
489.	The Last Straw		
490.	The Bounder's Way		
491.	Sir Jimmy's Pal	Spadger of the Slums	
492.	Sharing the Risk		
493.	Against His Own Side	Featuring Highcliffe	
494.	A Lesson for Skinner		
495.	On the Wrong Track	Roland Smale, 'tec	*ss E.S. Brooks*
496.	Hurree Singh's Secret	Kuri Din of St Jude's	
497.	Parted Pals		
498.	The Greyfriars Organiser		
499.	On the Make		*ss J.N. Pentelow*
500.	The Schoolboy Inventor	Sly Bill and Nutty Nat	*ss R.S. Kirkham*
501.	Judge Jeffreys	The Barring Out against Judge Jeffreys	
502.	Getting Out of Hand		
503.	The Greyfriars Inquisition		
504.	The Barring-Out at Greyfriars		
505.	Victory		
506.	Rivals of the Chase	Jack Archer	*ss G.R. Samways*

No.	Date	Title	Notes	
507.		**Ponsonby's Pal**	Ponsonby's feud	
508.		**Coker the Rebel**		
509.		**A Gentleman Ranker**	Jack Brown	*ss G.R. Samways*
510.		**An Old Boy at Greyfriars**	Levison, return to Greyfriars featuring	
511.		**Saving the Bounder**	Vernon Smith	
512.		**The Missing Skipper**		
513.		**The Greyfriars Christmas Party**	Double Christmas Number	*ss J.N. Pentelow*
514.		**Four from the East**	Featuring Wun Lung, Piet Delarey and Co.	*ss J.N. Pentelow*
515.		**Flap's Brother**	Flip and Flap Derwent	
516.		**Looking After Inky**	Featuring Kuri Din	
517.	5 - 1 - 1918	**In Another's Place**	Clavering of the Remove	
518.		**Clavering of the Remove**	Arrival of Tom Redwing	
519.		**The Whip Hand**		
520.		**A Very Gallant Gentleman**	Courtney of the Sixth dies	*ss J.N. Pentelow*
521.		**Danger Ahead**	Clavering continued	
522.		**Tom Redwing's Resolve**		
523.		**Hunting for Treasure**		*ss R.S. Kirkham*
524.		**Loyal Sir Jimmy**		*ss J.N. Pentelow*
525		**Skinner the Spy**		
526.		**Bunter's Latest**	Herr Gans	
527.		**A Bird of Passage**	Archie Drake	*ss G.R. Samways*
528.		**Coker the Joker**		
529.		**The Fighting Fifth**		*ss G.R. Samways*
530.		**Tom Redwing's Chance**	Tom Redwing's return	
531.		**Tom Redwing, Hero**		
532.		**Bunter to the Rescue**		

533.	**Tom Redwing's Win**		
534.	**Saved from Shame**	Featuring Ogilvy	
535.	**A Soldier's Son**	Roy Malcolm	*ss G.R. Samways*
536.	**The Man from the Somme**	Mr Snoop, deserter	
537.	**His Father's Son**		
538.	**Billy Bunter's Birthright**		*ss G.R. Samways*
539.	**Bolsover's Way**	Elliott leaves Greyfriars	
540.	**Napoleon of Greyfriars**	Intro. Napoleon Dupont	
541.	**William the Good**		
542.	**Bolsover's Enemy**		
543.	**Tom Redwing's Father**	Tom Redwing finds his father	
544.	**William the Warlike**		*ss G.R. Samways*
545.	**The Shylock of the Second**		*ss J.N. Pentelow*
546.	**Angel of the Fourth**	Angel of the Fourth's first appearance	
547.	**Kicking Over the Traces**		
548.	**Sir Jimmy's Enemy**		
549.	**The Second Form Mystery**		*ss J.N. Pentelow*
550.	**Put to the Test**		*ss G.R. Samways*
551.	**Coker's Campaign**		
552.	**Dick Russell's Chum**		*ss G.R. Samways*
553.	**Smithy's Scheme**	Redwing versus the Bounder series	
554.	**The Broken Bond**		
555.	**Rough on Redwing**		
556.	**Fallen Fortunes**		
557.	**The Greyfriars Tree Dwellings**	'Jawbones' Miller peace crank	*ss R.S. Kirkham*
558.	**The Missing Masterpiece**	Featuring Hopkins of the Shell	
559.	**A Case of Conscience**	Arrival of Richard Hilary	
560.	**His Country's Call**		

561.		**Coker's Latest**		*ss G.R. Samways*
562.		**Walker of the Sixth**		
563.		**In Spite of Himself**	Featuring Snoop	
564.		**Spring's Brother**		*ss J.N. Pentelow*
565.		**Sacked!**		*ss J.N. Pentelow*
566.		**The Wiles of Wibley**	Samuel Benson, new boy	*ss Will Gibbons*
567.		**Samuel and Sammy**		*ss J.N. Pentelow*
568.		**Bunter the Punter**	Wally Bunter at Greyfriars series	
569.	4 - 1 - 1919	**Wally Bunter's Luck**		
570.		**Billy Bunter's Wheeze**		
571.		**Wally of the Remove**		
572.		**A Dog with a Bad Name**		
573.		**The Amazing Bunter**		*ss J.N. Pentelow*
574.		**Bravo, Bunter!**		
575.		**For Another's Sins**		
576.		**The Black Sheep of Highcliffe**		
577.		**When Rogues Fall Out**		
578.		**Standing by Snoop**		
579.		**Wally's Wheeze**		
580.		**Hoskin's Chance**	Billy Bunter goes to St Jim's	
581.		**Giants at Grips**	Interluded St Jim's story	*ss G.R. Samways*
582.		**The Artful Dodger**		
583.		**Loder's Luck**		
584.		**The Terrible Uncle**		
585.		**The Return of the Native**		
586.		**Foes of the Remove**	Bolsover against Napoleon	
587.		**Missing from School**		

588.	**His Majesty the Major**		*ss G.R. Samways*
589.	**Treasure Trove**	Bunter's Auctioning Treasure series	
590.	**Bunter's Auction**		
591.	**Weggie of the Remove**		*ss F.G. Cook*
592.	**Billy Bunter's Bank Holiday**		*ss G.R. Samways*
593.	**Bunter the Bolshevik**		
594.	**The Greyfriars Swimming Sports**		*ss G.R. Samways*
595.	**Bessie versus Billy**		*ss G.R. Samways*
596.	**Linley's Legacy**		*ss W.L. Catchpole*
597.	**Catching Coker**		
598.	**The Great Bunter Mystery**		*ss C.M. Down*
599.	**Bunter's Aunt Sally**		*ss F.G. Cook*
600.	**The Hero's Homecoming**	Mr Lascelles returns from war service	
601.	**The Greyfriars Tourists**	The Famous Five's Tour of Belgium	*ss C.M. Down*
602.	**Schoolboys Abroad**		*ss C.M. Down*
603.	**Bunter's Typing Agency**		*ss G.R. Samways*
604.	**The Twelve Stamps**		*ss C.M. Down*
605.	**The Golden Clue**		*ss C.M. Down*
606.	**Sports Day at Greyfriars**		*ss G.R. Samways*
607.	**The Schoolboy Barber**		*ss C.M. Down*
608.	**The Secret of the Wires**		*ss C.M. Down*
609.	**The Greyfriars Detectives**	Ram Kudi and Inky	*ss N.W. Smith*
610.	**The Mystery of Mr Quelch**		*ss G.R. Samways*
611.	**Hurree Singh's Surprise Packet**		*ss R.S. Kirkham*
612.	**The Herald's Rival**		
613.	**The Bounder's Fault**	Featuring Vernon Smith	
614.	**Facing the Music**		

615.		**The Right Thing**		
616.		**Cast Out by His Chums**		*ss G.R. Samways*
617.		**The Rise and Fall of William Gosling**		
618.		**Alonzo's Agency**		*ss F.G. Cook*
619.		**Bunter on the Boards**		*ss N.W. Smith*
620.		**Bunter's Christmas Portrait**		*ss C.M. Down*
621.	3 - 1 - 1920	**The Terror in Black**		*ss J.N. Pentelow*
622.		**The Bounder's Farewell**	Smithy in Exile	*ss G.R. Samways*
623.		**Exiled from School**		*ss G.R. Samways*
624.		**Vernon Smith's Return**		*ss G.R. Samways*
625.		**Vernon Smith's Victory**		*ss G.R. Samways*
626.		**The Jape of the Term**		*ss F.G. Cook*
627.		**Smouldering Fires**		*ss G.R. Samways*
628.		**Phyllis Howell's Brother**		*ss G.R. Samways*
629.		**Squiff's Secret**		*ss J.N. Pentelow*
630.		**The Hold-Up at Greyfriars**		*ss C.M. Down*
631.		**The Silent Strike**		*ss N.W. Smith*
632.		**Mauleverer's Mission**		*ss Julius Herman*
633.		**Bob Cherry's Secret**	Jimmy Travers	*ss G.R. Samways*
634.		**The Blindness of Bunter**		*ss F.G. Cook*
635.		**The Feud With Friardale**		*ss G.R. Samways*
636.		**The Circus Hero**	Captain Punter	*ss Julius Herman*
637.		**Cup Tie Champions**		*ss G.R. Samways*
638.		**The Prefect's Predicament**		*ss F.G. Cook*
639		**The Scholarship Company**		
640		**Bunter the Bankrupt**		*ss Julius Herman*
641.		**The Invasion of Greyfriars**	Greyfriars under repair series	*ss G.R. Samways*

642.	Chums Awheel		*ss G.R. Samways*
643.	Billy Bunter's Speculation		
644.	Bunter the Farmer		*ss C.M. Down*
645.	The Greyfriars Minstrels		*ss Hedley O'Mant*
646.	Fun in the Fifth	Appearance of Phyllis and	*ss G.R. Samways*
647.	The Remove's Recruit	Archie Howell	*ss G.R. Samways*
648.	Her Brother's Honour		
649.	Chumming with Loder		
650.	A Third Form Mystery		*ss J.N. Pentelow*
651.	Bunter's Bluff		
652.	Bunter's Baby	original story:	*Charles Hamilton*
		rewritten:	*H.A. Hinton*
653.	The Schoolboy Artist	Teddy Teniel, new boy	*ss G.R. Samways*
654.	A Bid for the Captaincy		*ss S. Barrie*
655.	Archie Howell's Return		*ss G.R. Samways*
656.	In Borrowed Plumes		*ss C.M. Down*
657.	A False Hero		*ss S. Barrie*
658.	Loder's Luck		*ss S. Barrie*
659.	The Council of Action	Highcliffe Masters at Greyfriars	*ss S. Barrie*
660.	The Schoolboy Cinema Stars	The Greyfriars Film Stars	
661.	Wingate's Sacrifice		
662.	Her Schoolboy Chum	Wingate's Love affair	
663.	The Shadow of Shame		
664.	His Last Card		
665.	Coker's Craze		*ss F.G. Cook*
666.	The Man from America		*ss G.R. Samways*
667.	The Caterpillar's Rest Cure		*ss G.R. Samways*

No.	Date	Title	Notes	Author
668.		Smithy's Defiance		*ss S. Austin*
669.		Duping the Duffer		*ss F.G. Cook*
670.		Up Against It	Mr Hobbinson, new master	*ss J.N.' Pentelow*
671.		A Son's Dilemma		*ss N.W. Smith*
672.		Harry Wharton's Trust	Double Christmas Number Jerrold Drew-MacAlpine	
673.	1 - 1 - 1921	Ponsonby's Victim	Sir Timothy Topham	*ss G.R. Samways*
674.		The Runaway's Return		*ss G.R. Samways*
675.		Driven from School	Smithy Runs Away	*ss F.G. Cook*
676.		His Blundering Best		*ss J.N. Pentelow*
677.		Billy Bunter's Smugglers		*ss W.E.S. Hope*
678.		Scaring the School		*ss F.G. Cook*
679.		Harry Wharton's Sacrifice		*ss S.E. Austin*
680.		The Form Master's Disgrace	Mr Quelch in Disgrace	*ss W.E.S. Hope*
681.		By Wingate's Aid		*ss W.E.S. Hope*
682		Thin Bunter	Dick Rodney, Jack Drake featured	
683.		The Schoolboy Protectors	Edward Blundell	*ss F.G. Cook*
684.		Bunter the Swot		*ss G.R. Samways*
685.		Rivals of the River		*ss N.W. Smith*
686.		Marooned!		*ss S.E. Austin*
687.		Waking Up Alonzo		*ss G.R. Samways*
688.		Skinner's Secret Society		*ss G.R. Samways*
689.		Deaf Bunter		
690.		Bob Cherry's Luck	The Mr Jamfrey's series	*ss J.N. Pentelow*
691.		The Schoolboy Filmstars		*ss J.N. Pentelow*
692.		Mauleverer's Peril		*ss L.E. Ransome*
693.		Bunter's Picnic		

694.	The Vengeance of Woo Fing		*ss N.W. Smith*
695.	Wun Lung's Feud		*ss F.G. Cook*
696.	Sportsmen from the North		*ss G.R. Samways*
697.	Sleepers of the Remove		*S. Ross Shepherd*
698.	The Houseboat Mystery		*ss S.E. Austin*
699.	Bunter the Bandit		*ss F.G. Cook*
700.	Coker's Conquest		*ss G.R. Samways*
701.	Billy Bunter's Luck		*ss G.R. Samways*
702.	The Skipper's Bat		*ss J.N. Pentelow*
703.	The Society for Reforming Billy Bunter		*ss G.R. Samways*
704.	The Greyfriars Caravanners	Harry Wharton & Co on a caravan tour	
705.	The Secret of the Caravan		
706.	Mauly and the Caravanners		
707.	The Caravan Detective		
708.	Caravanners Afloat		
709.	Greyfriars Caravanners Abroad		
710.	Champion of the Remove		*ss G.R. Samways*
711.	Bunter the Bard		*ss G.R. Samways*
712.	The Island Raiders		*ss G.R. Samways*
713.	The Remove Exam Mystery		*ss S. Ross Shepherd*
714.	Skinner's Revenge		*ss R.J. Barnard*
715.	Bunter's Very Latest		
716.	The Plot Against the School	Jack Vernon, Old Boy	*ss G.R. Samways*
717.	The Stolen Guy		*ss N.W. Smith*
718.	The Slacker's Spasm	Dennis Carr	*ss G.R. Samways*
719.	Mark Linley's Trial		*ss F.G. Cook*
720.	Penfold Cuts Loose	Penfold cuts loose	*ss W.E. Hope*

721.		**Penfold the Blade**		*ss W.E. Hope*
722.		**Back to the Fold**		*ss W.E. Hope*
723.		**The Mystery of the Christmas Candles**		
724.		**Faithful to His Friend**		*ss G.R. Samways*
725.		**Against the Law**	Napoleon Dupont	*ss L. E. Ransome*
726.	7 - 1 - 1922	**The Team That Couldn't Be Beaten**	Jack Cromwell	*ss G.R. Samways*
727.		**The Footballers Feud**	Dr Armstrong series	*ss S.Ross Shepherd*
728.		**Wibley the Wonder**		*ss S.Ross Shepherd*
729.		**Billy Bunter's Big Bargain**		
730.		**The Remove Rugger Team**		
731.		**Mr Bunter – Form Master**	Wally Bunter as Form Master	*ss G.R. Samways*
732.		**The Bunters' Conspiracy**		*ss G.R. Samways*
733.		**The Mystery of the Warning**		*ss G.R. Samways*
734.		**A Form Master's Fate**		*ss G.R. Samways*
735.		**Wally Wins Through**		*ss G.R. Samways*
736.		**Billy Bunter Filmstar**		*ss W.E. Pike*
737.		**Bunter's Bolt**		
738.		**Hunting Bunter**	Billy Bunter, runaway	
739.		**Bagging Bunter**		
740.		**The Greyfriars Exile**		*ss S.Ross Shepherd*
741.		**His Excellency, Count Bunter**		*ss S.Ross Shepherd*
742.		**Tickets for the Final**		*ss W.E.S. Hope*
743.		**When The Head Resigned**	The Sixth Form rebellion	
744.		**The Sixth Form Rebellion**		
745.		**The Greyfriars Barring Out**		
746.		**The Stolen Diary**	Smithy's Diary	*ss S.E. Austin*
747.		**For His Father's Name**		*ss S.E. Austin*

No.	Title	Notes	Author
748.	Bunter the Crook		
749.	De Vere of the Remove	Algernon de Vere series	
750.	The Snob's Secret		
751.	In Borrowed Plumes		
752.	The Fall of Algernon		
753.	Bunter's Raffle		
754.	Bravo, Bulstrode!		*ss G.R. Samways*
755.	Mauly's Pals		
756.	The Mysterious Foe	A Yachting tour with Mauly to France	
757.	The Schoolboy Yachtsman		
758.	The Mystery of the Silver Scud		
759.	The Terror Tracked Down		
760.	Coker's Rival		
761.	Skinner's Chum		
762.	The Schoolboy Divers	Captain Holden	*ss N.W. Smith*
763.	The Persecution of Mr Prout		
764.	Fishy the Footballer	Fishy's attempt to enter the Remove XI	
765.	The Footballer's Foe		
766.	Loder's Long Trail		
767.	Bunter's Lawsuit		*ss F.G. Cook*
768.	The Man from the Congo	Harry Wharton and Co with	
769.	Bound for Africa	Captain Cockran in Africa	
START OF THE COLOURED COVER			
770.	Harry Wharton & Co in Africa		
771.	Lost in the Congo		
772.	King Bunter of the Congo		
773.	On the Ivory Trail		

774.		**The Black Man at Greyfriars**		*ss N.W. Smith*
775.		**The Call from the Air**		
776.		**The Ghost of Mauleverer Towers**		
777.		**Ponsonby's Revenge**		*ss F.G. Cook*
778.	6–1–1923	**The Jap of Greyfriars**		*ss F.G. Cook*
779.		**The New Boy's Secret**	Jim Lee	
780.		**Detective Bunter**		*ss S.E. Austin*
781.		**The Schoolboy Hermit**	Jim Lee of the Remove	
782.		**Just Like Bunter**		
783.		**Straight as a Die**		
784.		**Friends at Last**		
785.		**Alonzo the Athlete**		*ss F.G. Cook*
786.		**The Sporting Champion**		*ss G.R. Samways*
787.		**Bunter's Latest**		
788.		**The Supreme Sacrifice**		*ss W.E.S. Hope*
789.		**Billy Bunter's Boat Race Party**		
790.		**A Message from the Sea**		*ss S.E. Austin*
791.		**The Jester of Greyfriars**		*ss G.R. Samways*
792.		**Rivals and Chums**		*ss F.G. Cook*
793.		**How Levison Minor came to Greyfriars**	Levison's return to Greyfriars	
794.		**The Boy with a Bad Name**		
795.		**Under the Shadow**		
796.		**A Friend in Need**		
797.		**A Debt Repaid**		
798.		**The Hand of the Enemy**		
799.		**Levison's Triumph**		
800.		**The Haunted Camp**		*ss G.R. Samways*

801.	**The Greyfriars Day Boarder**	Major Thresher	*ss G.R. Samways*
802.	**Bunter's Barring Out**		*ss F.G. Cook*
803.	**A Puzzle for the Remove**	The Willesby Twins	*ss J.N. Pentelow*
804.	**The Twin Tangle**		*ss J.N. Pentelow*
805.	**The Hand of Fate**		*ss J.N. Pentelow*
806.	**Lame Bunter**		
807.	**Mauleverer Means Business**		
808.	**A Split in the Co**		
809.	**Sir Jimmy's Substitute**	With Sir Jimmy Vivian at Pengarth, Cornwall	
810.	**Bunter the Hunter**		
811.	**The House of Pengarth**		
812.	**The Secret of the Caves**		
813.	**The Heart of a Hero**	Robert Annesly Seven dies	*ss G.R. Samways*
814.	**Montague the Mysterious**	Montague Snooks	
815.	**Fishy's Friendly Society**		*ss F.G. Cook*
816.	**An Island Mystery**	Mr Hart, detective	*ss S.E. Austin*
817.	**Condemned by the School**	Return of Cecil Snaith	*ss F.G. Cook*
818.	**Disgraced By His Father**	Sexton Blake	*ss N.W. Smith*
819.	**Mick the Outcast**	Mick the Gipsy	
820.	**The Gipsy Schoolboy**		
821.	**Mick the Untameable**		
822.	**The Luck of the Gipsy**		
823.	**The Gipsy Millionaire**		
824.	**The Greyfriars Gliding Competition**		*ss F.G. Cook*
825.	**The Coker Challenge Cup**	Jimmy Carfax	*ss G.R. Samways*
826.	**The Rebel of the Remove**		
827.	**True as Steel**		*ss G.R. Samways*

828.		**The Gipsy's Return**	Mick Angel's return (Mick the gipsy)	
829.		**The Phantom of the Highlands**		
830.	**5 - 1 - 1924**	**The Wraith of Lockmuir**		
831.		**The Greyfriars Newspaper**		*ss G.R. Samways*
832.		**The Waywardness of Wibley**		*ss S.E. Austin*
833.		**The Greyfriars Flood**		*ss S.R. Shepherd*
834.		**Coker's Brainwave**		
835.		**Mauly's Amazing Adventure**		*ss F.G. Cook*
836.		**Bunter's Poor Relations**		*ss G.R. Samways*
837.		**The White Feather**		*ss F.G. Cook*
838.		**The Young Pretender**		*ss G.R. Samways*
839.		**Duffer and Hero**		*ss G.R. Samways*
840.		**The Rebels of the Second**	Dr Craddock, new Headmaster	*ss F.G. Cook*
841.		**Fishy's Treasure**		
842.		**True to His Word**	Slinker Bates	*ss S.E. Austin*
843.		**Pen's Pal**		
844.		**The Plundered School**	Hon. James Maxwell Old Boy	*ss G.R. Samways*
845.		**Inky's Peril**		*ss F.G. Cook*
846.		**Too Clever of Skinner**		
847.		**The Secret of the Shark's Tooth**		*ss S.E. Austin*
848.		**The Barring of Bunter**		
849.		**Capped for Greyfriars**		*ss J.N. Pentelow*
850.		**The Outcast of The Remove**		*ss F.G. Cook*
851.		**The Iron Hand at Greyfriars**	Dr Sterndale – Major Thresher	*ss G.R. Samways*
852.		**Peter the Plotter**		
853.		**Standing by Their Pals**		
854.		**The Man Who Came Back**	Old Boy Philip Blagden and treasure	

855.	**Treasure Trove**		
856.	**Drummed out of Greyfriars**		*ss F.G. Cook*
857.	**The Schoolboy Domestics**		*ss Hedley O'Mant*
858.	**The Parting of the Ways**	Smithy versus Redwing feud	
859.	**Sentenced by the Form**		
860.	**Vernon Smith's Feud**		
861.	**True Blue**	Ted Thornton, new boy	*ss J.N. Pentelow*
862.	**The Greyfriars Arab**		
863.	**The Foe From Africa**		
864.	**Bound for Africa**	Harry Wharton and Co in the Sahara	
865.	**The Schoolboy Tourists**		
866.	**The Call of the Desert**		
867.	**Foes of the Sahara**		
868.	**In the Power of the Sheik**		
869.	**The Vengeance of the Sheik**		
870.	**Billy Bunter's Wembley Party**		*ss S.E. Austin*
871.	**Sir Hilton's Nephew**		*ss S.E. Austin*
872.	**The Mystery Wreck**		*ss S.E. Austin*
873.	**Both Bunters**	Last appearance of Wally Bunter	
874.	**Giving Bunter Beans**	The Bunking of Billy Bunter	
875.	**The Vanished Ventriloquist**		
876	**The Bunking of Bunter**		
877.	**Billy Bunter's Campaign**		
878.	**The Schoolboy Financier**		*ss F.G. Cook*
879.	**Trouble in the Co**	The first downfall series	
880.	**Harry Wharton's Christmas**		
881.	**Friends or Foes?**		

882.	3 - 1 - 1925	**The Downward Path**	Harry Wharton, Rebel	
883.		**The Rebel of the Remove**		
884.		**Slacker and Captain**		
885.		**Harry Wharton's Downfall**		
886.		**Down and Out**		
887.		**The Worst Boy at Greyfriars**		
888.		**Harry Wharton's Last Chance**		
889.		**To Shield His Father**	featuring Edwin Myers	*ss G.R. Samways*
890.		**The Barring of Bolsover**		*ss S.E. Austin*
891.		**The Great Postal Order Mystery**		*ss G.R. Samways*
892.		**Bunter the Prophet**		*ss G.R. Samways*
893.		**Coker's Crosswords**		
894.		**The Mystery of Mossoo**	Signor Tompionio	*ss F.G. Cook*
895.		**Aunt Judy Comes to Stay**		*ss F.G. Cook*
896.		**Poor Old Bunter!**		
897.		**Bunter the Cavalier**		
898.		**The Schoolboy Sculptor**		*ss S.E. Austin*
899.		**Playing the Goat**		
900.		**Buck Up, Bunter**		
901.		**'Pep' for the 'Friars**	Hiram K. Parks, new Head	*ss S.Ross Shepherd*
902.		**The Feud with Cliff House**		*ss F.G. Cook*
903.		**Sports Week at Greyfriars**		*ss G.R. Samways*
904.		**The Rival Tuckshops**		*ss S.E. Austin*
905.		**Alonzo the Slogger**		*ss S.Ross Shepherd*
906.		**Ragged Dick**	Ragged Dick Series	
907.		**Ragged Dick at Greyfriars**		
908.		**Ragged Dick's Resolve**		

909.		A Boy's Crossroads		
910.		Billy Bunter's Brainwave	Bunter Court series	
911.		Bunter of Bunter Court		
912.		Billy Bunter's Masterstroke		
913.		The Mystery of Bunter Court		
914.		The Bunter Court Eleven		
915.		The Prisoners of Bunter Court		
916.		Billy Bunter's Bolt		
917.		Bunter Caught		
918.		Rival Oarsmen	Major Thresher	*ss G.R. Samways*
919.		Schoolboy versus Pro's		*ss G.R. Samways*
920.		Fishy's Hair-raising Stunt		*ss F.G. Cook*
921.		The Greyfriars Film Fans		*ss S.R. Shepherd*
922.		The Bounder's Way		*ss S.E. Austin*
923.		Brother and Prefect	Gerald Loder, Captain series	
924.		The Scapegrace of the Third		
925.		His Brother's Burden		
926.		The Captain's Election		
927.		The Whip Hand		
928.		Captain and Tyrant		
929.		The Worst Form at Greyfriars		
930.		Rebels of Greyfriars.		
931.		Loder's Last Chance		
932.		Facing the World	Smith's father loses his fortune.	*ss S.R. Shepherd*
933.		From Greyfriars to Borstal	Smith leaves Greyfriars	*ss S.R. Shepherd*
934.	2 - 1 - 1926	Bowling Out Bunter		*ss S.E. Austin*
935.		Coker's New Year Resolution		*ss G.R. Samways*

936.	**Quelchy's Queer Adventure**	Rupert Villemond, Old Boy, French Canadian	*ss Hedley O'Mant*
937.	**The Prefect's Plot**		*ss Unknown*
938.	**The Hand of an Enemy**	Linley Expelled	*ss S.E. Austin*
939.	**Back to the Factory Again**		*ss S.E. Austin*
940.	**The Hidden Foe**		*ss S.E. Austin*
941.	**Billy Bunter's Legacy**		*ss H.W. Twyman*
942.	**The Mystery of the Head's Study**		
943.	**A Feud with the Fourth**		*ss Noel Wood Smith*
944.	**Fishy's Debt Collecting Agency**		*ss F.G. Cook*
945.	**A Star of the Circus**	Pedrillo of Zorro's Circus series	
946.	**Pedrillo of Greyfriars**		
947.	**The Circus Schoolboy**		
948.	**Righting a Wrong**		
949.	**The Temptation of Peter Hazeldene**		*ss H.W. Twyman*
950.	**The Ragging of Mossoo**	Mossoo ragging series	
951.	**Harry Wharton's Feud**		
952.	**The New Boy's Secret**	Wilfred Punter	*ss Kenneth Newman*
953.	**The Mystery of Popper's Island**	Walker's Aunt series	*ss S.E. Austin*
954.	**For Another's Sake**		*ss S.E. Austin*
955.	**Bunter's Treasure Trove**		*ss S.E. Austin*
956.	**The Persecution of Billy Bunter**	Bunter's Barring-In series	
957.	**Bunter's Barring-In**		
958.	**The Slacker's Awakening**	Famous Five and Ponsonby Feud	
959.	**The Punishment of Ponsonby**		
960.	**The Japer of Greyfriars**	Harry Wharton & Co in India	
961.	**The Nabob's Double**		

962.		**The Peril of the Night**		
963.		**Outward Bound**		
964.		**In Perilous Seas**		
965.		**Harry Wharton and Co in India**		
966.		**Bound for Bhanipur**		
967.		**In the Heart of the Himalayas**		
968.		**The Terror of the Jungle**		
969.		**The Nabob's Rival**		
970.		**From India to Greyfriars**		
971.		**Coker the Rebel**		
972.		**Chums Through Thick and Thin**		*ss Hedley O'Mant*
973.		**Asking for Trouble**		
974.		**The Suspected Form master**	Major Thresher	*ss G.R. Samways*
975.		**The Swot**	Bob Cherry, swot, against the Remove	
976,		**The Ishmael of the Form**		
977.		**The Deserter**		
978.		**Nobody's Chum**		
979.		**Bob Cherry Wins Through**		
980.		**Heroes of the Air**		*ss Hedley O'Mant*
981.		**Coker on the Warpath**	Coker and Mr Poyning – last mention	
982.		**Missing from School**	of Reggie Coker	
983.		**The Prisoner of the Bungalow**		
984.		**Coker's Christmas Party**		
985.	1 - 1 - 1927	**The Game Kid**	The Game Kid	
986.		**The Bruiser of the Remove**		
987.		**Bound by Honour**		
988.		**The Game Kid's Temptation**		

989.	**Loyal to the last**		
990.	**The Call of the Ring**		
991.	**The Schoolboy Broadcasters**		*ss A.W. Davis*
992.	**The Footprint in the Sand**		
993.	**Fishy's Travel Agency**		*ss A.W. Davis*
994.	**Roger of the Remove**	Roger Quelch series, Mr Quelch's	
995.	**Fed Up with Greyfriars**	nephew	
996.	**Bunter's Brainstorm**		
997.	**The Interloper**	Paul Dallas series	
998.	**The Bounder's Feud**		
999.	**Condemned by the Form**		
1000.	**Paying the Price**		
1001.	**The Hand of an Enemy**		
1002.	**At the End of His Tether**		
1003.	**The Complete Outsider**		
1004.	**The Boy Who Found His Father**		
1005.	**Bunter the Bold**		
1006.	**Fishy's Burglar Hunt**		*ss W.L. Catchpole*
1007.	**The Bounder's Win**	Captain Spencer series	
1008.	**One Against the School**		
1009.	**Hunted Down**		
1010.	**Taking Up Trotter**		
1011.	**Bolsover's Brother**		
1012.	**The Bounder's Good Turn**	Smithy against Wharton series	
1013.	**Smithy's Way**		
1014.	**Bunter the Bad Lad**		*ss Hedley O'Mant*
1015.	**Smithy's Pal**		

1016.	**Bravo. Bunter!**		
1017.	**The Man from the South Seas**	The South Seas series	
1018.	**The Treasure Chart**		
1019.	**Tom Redwing's Quest**	First appearance of James Soames	
1020.	**Bunter the Stowaway**		
1021.	**The Southern Seas**	Harry Wharton & Co with Smithy and Redwing	
1022.	**The Whip Hand**		
1023.	**The Treasure Island**		
1024.	**The Rival Treasure Seekers**		
1025.	**Black Peter's Treasure**		
1026.	**The Greyfriars Castaways**		
1027.	**Skinner Tries It On**		
1028.	**Tom Redwing's Return**	Edgar Bright	
1029.	**The Great Fifth at Greyfriars**		
1030.	**A Ventriloquist at Large**		*ss S.E. Austin*
1031.	**The Toad of the Remove**	Levison's Return	
1032.	**Levison Makes Good**		
1033.	**Sent to Coventry**		
1034.	**Levison's Luck**		
1035.	**The Prefect's Secret**		
1036.	**Bunter's Christmas Present**	Bunter the philanthropist	
1037.	**Bunter the Benovolent**		
1038. 7 - 1 - 28	**The Mystery of Wharton Lodge**		
1039.	**Billy Bunter's Convict**	Edgar Gilmore, Second form-master	
1040.	**Convict Nineteen**		
1041.	**The Form Master's Foe**		
1042.	**The Fellow Who Wouldn't Be Caned**		

1043.	**Dismissed from Greyfriars**	The 'High Oaks' Rebellion series	
1044.	**Rebellion of the Remove**		
1045.	**The School Without a Master**		
1046.	**High Jinks at High Oaks**		
1047.	**Mutiny**		
1048.	**The Boy Headmaster**		
1049.	**The Return of the Rebels**		
1050.	**Black Magic**	Crum, the schoolboy hypnotist	
1051.	**The Schoolboy Hypnotist**		
1052.	**The New Boy's Enemy**		
1053.	**In Merciless Hands**		*ss Hedley O'Mant*
1054.	**Bunter's Prize Essay**		*ss W.L. Catchpole*
1055.	**Coker's League of Friends**		*ss Hedley O'Mant*
1056.	**Billy Bunter's Bike**	The De Courcy bicycle series	
1057.	**For the Honour of Greyfriars**		
1058.	**The Hero of the Fifth**		*ss W.L. Catchpole*
1059.	**The Boy from the East**	Arthur Da Costa series	
1060.	**Friend or Foe**		
1061.	**By Luck and Pluck**		
1062.	**The Schemer of the Remove**		
1063.	**Harry Wharton's Enemy**		
1064.	**Playing the Game**		
1065.	**Tried and True**		
1066.	**In Borrowed Plumes**		
1067.	**A Fortune at Stake**		
1068.	**Billy Bunter's Bookmaker**		
1069.	**Billy Bunter's Luck**	Whiffles' Circus	

1070.		Bunter the Boss		
1071.		Billy Bunter's Circus		
1072.		Bunter's Big Bluff		
1073.		Bunter's Bodyguard		
1074.		Chums of the Circus		
1075.		The Order of the Boot		
1076.		Bunter Comes to Stay		
1077.		Secret of the Schooner		*ss Hedley O'Mant*
1078.		The Japer of Greyfriars	Christopher Clarence Carboy	
1079.		Be Careful, Christopher		
1080.		The Boy With a Past		
1081.		Rallying Round Carboy		
1082.		All Through Bunter		
1083.		Shunned by the Form		*ss Hedley O'Mant*
1084.		The Rebel of the Fifth	Coker suspected of punching Prout series	
1085.		Who Punched Prout?		
1086.		The Form Master's Feud		
1087.		The Phantom of the Cave	Phantom of the cave, featuring	
1088.		The Clue of the Coral Knife	James Soames	
1089.		Hunted Down		
1090.	5 - 1 - 1929	Under Bunter's Thumb		
1091.		Bunter – Big Game Hunter		*ss S.E. Austin*
1092.		From School to Hollywood	Harry Wharton and Co in Hollywood	
1093.		Bound for America		
1094.		Harry Wharton & Co in New York		
1095.		Greyfriars Chums in Chicago		
1096.		Held Up by Bandits		
1097.		Bunter's Amazing Adventure		

1098.	**Harry Wharton & Co in Hollywood**	
1099.	**Billy Bunter on the Films**	
1100.	**The Hero of Hollywood**	
1101.	**The Bootleggers' Revenge**	
1102.	**The Filmstars' Feud**	
1103.	**The Schoolboy Sheik**	
1104.	**Harry Wharton's Peril**	
1105.	**A Filmstar's Vengeance**	
1106.	**All Through Bunter**	
1107.	**Farewell to the Films**	
1108.	**The Masked Terror**	*ss Hedley O'Mant*
1109.	**Billy Bunter's Blunder**	*ss Hedley O'Mant*
1110.	**The Shylock of Greyfriars**	
1111.	**The Prefects' Plot**	Wingate versus Loder series
1112.	**Prefects at War**	
1113.	**Out of Bounds**	Loder versus Famous Five series
1114.	**The Black Sheep of the Sixth**	
1115.	**A Lesson for Loder**	
1116.	**The Mystery of Mark Linley**	Linley suspected of stealing ten pounds
1117.	**Under Suspicion**	
1118.	**Bob Cherry's Big Bargain**	August holiday walking tour – the
1119.	**The Trail of the Trike**	mystery of the trike.
1120.	**Chums on the Tramp**	
1121.	**The Mystery of the Methuselah**	
1122.	**The House of Terror**	The Mystery of Ravenspur Grange
1123.	**The Unseen Foe**	
1124.	**The Mystery of the Grange**	

1125.		**The Terror Tracked Down**	
1126.		**The Boy Without a Friend**	Julian Delvarney
1127.		**Monty Newland's Enemy**	
1128.		**The New Boy's Feud**	
1129.		**Coker Comes a Cropper**	
1130.		**A Rogue in the Remove**	Arthur Durance (new boy) series
1131.		**The Schoolboy Detective**	
1132.		**Skinner's Shady Scheme**	
1133.		**Blackmail**	Mr Prout blackmailed
1134.		**Fool's Luck**	
1135.		**Coward's Courage**	
1136.		**Six in the Soup**	
1137.		**Bunter the Bandit**	
1138.		**Coker's Cracksman**	The Courtfield Cracksman series
1139.		**Quelchy's Christmas Present**	
1140.		**Billy Bunter's Christmas**	
1141.		**Bunter Comes to Stay**	
1142.	4 - 1 - 1930	**The Artful Dodger**	
1143.		**The Formmaster's Favourite**	
1144.		**Wanted by the Police**	
1145.		**The Mystery Master**	
1146.		**Some Person Unknown**	
1147.		**Billy Bunter's Bluff**	
1148.		**The Man From Scotland Yard**	
1149.		**Goodbye Bunter**	
1150.		**The Greyfriars Cracksman**	
1151.		**Billy Bunter's Comeback**	

1152.	**Nap of the Remove**		*ss Hedley O'Mant*
1153.	**Greasepaint Wibley**		*ss Hedley O'Mant*
1154.	**The Fool of the Fifth**	Coker in First Eleven series	
1155.	**Duffer and Hero**		
1156.	**Who Hacked Hacker?**		
1157.	**The Mystery of the Silver Box**	Missing moonstone series	
1158.	**The Missing Moonstone**		
1159.	**Bunter the Prize Hunter**		
1160.	**Bunter the Ink Splasher**		
1161.	**Rolling in Dollars**	Gangsters at Greyfriars	
1162.	**Gangsters at Greyfriars**		
1163.	**The Hold Up at Greyfriars**		
1164.	**Catching Fish**		
1165.	**The Mystery of the Poplars**		
1166.	**Pop of the Circus**	Pop of the Circus	
1167.	**Waking up Greyfriars**		
1168.	**The Call of the Circus**		
1169.	**The Hidden Hand**	The Remove rebellion against Mr Brandon	
1170.	**Tale-bearer in Chief**		
1171.	**The Greyfriars Rebellion**		
1172.	**Down with the Tyrant!**		
1173.	**All Busy on the Greyfriars Front**		
1174.	**Victory for the Rebels**		
1175.	**The Menace of Tang Wang**	The China series (Tang Wang)	
1176.	**The Peril from the East**		
1177.	**The Foe from the Sky**		
1178.	**All Aboard for China**		

1179.		The Hand of the Mandarin	
1180.		The Terror of the Tong	The China series (Tang Wang) contd.
1181.		The Scourge of the Red Dragon	
1182.		Greyfriars Chums in China	
1183.		The Mandarin's Vengeance	
1184.		The Beggar of Shantung	
1185.		The City of Death	
1186.		Saved from the Sea	
1187.		Prout's Lovely Black Eye	Prout's Black Eye series
1188.		Who Punched Prout?	
1189.		Skinner's Narrow Squeak	*ss Hedley O'Mant*
1190.		The Schoolboy Form Master	
1191.		Billy Bunter's Christmas	The mystery of Cavandale Abbey
1192.		The Mystery of Cavandale Abbey	
1193.		The Phantom of the Abbey	
1194.	3 - 1 - 1931	The Secret Sniper	
1195.		The Boy Without a Name	'Tatters' of the Remove
1196.		Chumley for Short	
1197.		The Mystery of the Paper Chase	
1198.		Tatters of the Remove	
1199.		Chivvying Chumley	
1200.		The Voice of the Tempter	
1201.		The Amateur Rogue	
1202.		The Rogue's Remorse	
1203.		A Kinsman's Treachery	
1204.		The Champion Chump	
1205.		A Schoolboy's Sacrifice	

1206.	**Billy Bunter's Bunk**	
1207.	**The Man from the States**	
1208.	**The Mystery of the Mill**	
1209.	**Coker's Holiday Capture**	The Lancaster series
1210.	**Coker's Desperate Adventure**	
1211.	**Cracksman and Cricketer**	
1212.	**Foes of the Sixth**	
1213.	**The Schoolboy Cracksman**	
1214.	**The Shadow of the Underworld**	
1215.	**The Greyfriars Pretender**	
1216	**Unmasked**	
1217.	**The Boy Who Knew Too Much**	
1218.	**The Way of the Wizard**	
1219.	**Bandits on the Line**	
1220.	**Speedway Coker**	*ss M. Duffy.*

EVERY STORY AFTER THIS DATE WAS WRITTEN BY CHARLES HAMILTON

1221.	**Billy Bunter's Bargain**	
1222.	**Bluffing the Beak**	The Bounder expelled series
1223.	**The Impossible Schooling**	
1224.	**The Night Raiders**	The Secret of the Oak series
1225.	**The Secret of the Oak**	
1226.	**Billy Bunter's Hat Trick**	
1227.	**A Dog With a Bad Name**	
1228.	**The Schoolboy Lion Hunters**	Harry Wharton & Co in Africa with Smithy
1229.	**Jungle Vengeance**	

1230.		The Jungle Hikers	
1231.		Kidnapped in Kenya	
1232.		The Man Tracker of Uganda	
1233.		The Slave Trader's Vengeance	
1234.		White Slaves of the Congo	
1235.		The City of Terror	
1236.		Saved from the Cannibals	
1237.		Widgers on the Warpath	
1238.		All the Fun of the Fifth	
1239.		The Boot Boy's Luck	
1240.		Foes of the Remove	
1241.		Coker's Football Fever	
1242.		The Bounder's Blunder	
1243.		A Brother's Sacrifice	
1244.		The Ghost of Mauleverer Towers	Christmas at Mauleverer Towers
1245.		The Unknown Hand	
1246.	2 - 1 - 1932	The Secret of the Turrett	
1247.		Bunter's Night Out	Flip of the Second series
1248.		The Terror of the Form	
1249.		Billy Bunter's Cert.	
1250.		Bold Bad Bunter	
1251.		The Schoolmaster Cracksman	
1252.		Jimmy the One	
1253.		The Hunted Master	
1254.		While Greyfriars Slept	
1255.		The Complete Outsider	Harry Wharton down on his luck
1256.		Down on His Luck	

No.	Title	Notes
1257.	Harry Wharton's Downfall	
1258.	Bounder and Captain	
1259.	The Swot of the Remove	
1260.	The Bounder's Folly	
1261.	Harry Wharton's Enemy	
1262.	The Fool of the School	
1263	The Vanished Sovereigns	
1264.	The Bounder's Luck	All complete stories with The Bounder as captain
1265.	Billy Bunter's Vengeance	
1266.	Saving His Enemy	
1267.	Coker's Cricket Craze	
1268.	The Secret of the Priory	
1269.	Truants of the Remove	
1270.	Coker's Camera Clicks	
1271.	The Mystery of No 1 Study	The Green Sachel series
1272.	Hidden Plunder	
1273.	Coker the Champion Chump	
1274.	Billy Bunter's Banknote	
1275.	The Mystery of the Green Sachel	
1276.	Who Walloped Wiggins?	
1277.	Billy Bunter's Bad Luck	
1278.	Southward Bound	Harry Wharton and Co in Egypt
1279.	Harry Wharton and Co in Egypt	
1280.	The Lure of the Golden Scarab	
1281.	Billy Bunter's Bargain	
1282.	The Shadowed Schoolboy	
1283.	The Secret of the Scarab	

1284.		The Eye of the Osiris	
1285.		The Worst Boy in the Form	Harry Wharton versus Mr Quelch
1286.		The Rebel of the Remove	
1287.		Harry Wharton Declares War	
1288.		The Schemer of the Sixth	
1289.		The Way of the Rebel	
1290.		The Glorious Fifth at Greyfriars	
1291.		Hunting for Trouble	
1292.		The Scapegrace of the School	
1293.		Nobody's Pal	
1294.		The Spy of the Sixth	
1295.		Saved by a Scapegrace	
1296.		The Runaway Rebel	
1297.		The Boy from the Underworld	Dick the Penman series
1298.		The Kidnapped Schoolboy	(Jim Valentine, alias Dick the Penman)
1299.	7 - 1 - 1933	Dick the Penman	
1300.		The Boy With a Guilty Secret	
1301.		His Past Against Him	
1302.		Coker the Detective	
1303.		Bunter the Footballer	
1304.		The Mad Musicians at Greyfriars	
1305.		Black Magic	
1306.		Billy Bunter's Bargains	
1307.		The Hunted Schoolboy	
1308.		Wibley's Wonderful Wheeze	
1309.		Popper's Unpopular Prize	
1310.		The Schoolboy Impersonator	

1311.	**All Through Bunter**	
1312.	**Billy Bunter's Easter Cruise**	Billy Bunter's Easter cruise
1313.	**The Greyfriars Chums Afloat**	
1314.	**Saved from the Sea**	
1315.	**The Schoolboy Tourists**	
1316.	**Bunter's Big Bluff**	
1317.	**After Lights Out**	
1318.	**Taming a Tyrant**	
1319.	**The Deserter**	Vernon Smith sent to Coventry
1320.	**Barred By His Form**	
1321.	**The Boxing Beak**	Mr Lascelles disappears
1322.	**The Kidnapped Master**	
1323.	**The Worst Boy in the School**	
1324.	**Aunt Judy at Greyfriars**	
1325.	**Bunter's £100 Boater**	Bunter's boater hat series
1326.	**Billy Bunter's Hat Trick**	
1327.	**The Shylock of Greyfriars**	
1328.	**Bunter the Ventriloquist**	
1329.	**The Bounder's Good Turn**	
1330.	**The Millionaire Detective**	Greyfriars hikers series
1331.	**Micky the Sprat**	
1332.	**The Greyfriars Hikers**	
1333.	**Down on the Farm**	
1334.	**The Hunted Hikers**	
1335.	**The Spectre of Hoad Castle**	
1336.	**Coker the Hiker**	
1337.	**The Kidnapped Hiker**	

1338.		**The Hiker's Prisoner**	
1339.		**The Bounder's Capture**	
1340.		**The Secret of the Holiday Annual**	
1341.		**The Ace of Jokers**	
1342.		**The Greyfriars Guy**	
1343.		**Down With the Tyrant**	
1344.		**The Greyfriars Strong Man**	Strong man Alonzo
1345.		**Alonzo the Great**	
1346.		**The Greyfriars Hercules**	
1347.		**The Reformer of the Remove**	
1348.		**Bunter the Bully**	
1349.		**The Mystery of Wharton Lodge**	Bunter's diamond series
1350.		**The Ghost of Wharton Lodge**	
1351.	6 - 1 - 1934	**Bunter the Masher**	
1352.		**Billy Bunter's Diamond**	
1353.		**The Profiteer of the Remove**	
1354.		**Kidnapped from the Air**	Bob Cherry kidnapped
1355.		**The Mystery of the Vaults**	
1356.		**The Bounder's Folly**	
1357.		**The Vanished Schoolboys**	
1358.		**The Slacker's Awakening**	
1359.		**Who Walloped Wingate?**	
1360.		**The Mystery of the Head's Hat**	The Smedley series
1361.		**Disowned By His Father**	
1362.		**The Bounder's Rival**	
1363.		**The Form Master's Secret**	
1364.		**Form Master and Rogue**	

1365.	The Bounder's Big Bluff	
1366.	The Schoolboy Trippers	
1367.	The Shadowed Schoolboy	
1368.	The Spying Form Master	
1369.	Bunter the Ventriloquist	
1370.	Saving a Scapegrace	
1371.	The Bounder's Sacrifice	
1372.	The Worst Master in the School	
1373.	Rivals for a Fortune	
1374.	The Bunking of Billy Bunter	The Popper Island rebellion
1375.	Backing up Bunter	
1376.	Bunter the Dodger	
1377.	In Open Revolt	
1378.	The Island Schoolboys	
1379.	The No-Surrender Schoolboys	
1380.	The Secret of the Old Oak	
1381.	Fishy's Fearful Fix	
1382.	The Rebels at Bay	
1383.	Bunter the Billionaire	The Billionaire series
1384.	A Snob in Clover	
1385.	Billionairing with Bunter	
1386.	The Shadowed Billionaire	
1387.	Bagged by Bandits	
1388.	Ructions in Rome	
1389.	Peril in the Air	
1390.	A Tyrant Rules Greyfriars	The Greyfriars Secret Society
1391.	The High Hand	

1392.		**The Greyfriars Stormtroopers**	
1393.		**The Secret of the Vaults**	
1394.		**The Secret Seven**	
1395.		**Fooled on the Fifth**	
1396.		**The Dictator of Greyfriars**	
1397.		**The Brotherhood of Justice**	
1398.		**A Traitor in the Camp**	
1399		**The Schoolboy Sleuth**	
1400.		**Putting Paid to Prout**	Christmas at Hilton Hall
1401.		**Christmas at Hilton Hall**	
1402.		**Hunted Down**	
1403.	5 - 1 - 1935	**The Fugitive of the Moor**	
1404.		**Coker's Cousin Comes to Greyfriars**	Coker's cousin, Edgar Caffyn
1405.		**The Mischief-Maker of the Remove**	
1406.		**Down on His Luck**	
1407.		**Fools Luck**	
1408.		**The Schemer of the Remove**	
1409.		**The Remove's Remarkable Recruit**	
1410.		**The Unseen Witness**	
1411.		**The Fifth Form Mystery**	
1412.		**Coker the Reformer**	
1413.		**A Schoolboy's Secret**	Hazeldine's Uncle
1414.		**Honours Even**	
1415.		**The Sleuth of Greyfriars**	
1416.		**Fooled on the First**	
1417.		**Facing the Music**	
1418.		**Quelch's Easter Egg**	

1419.	**Jimmy the Fox**	Jimmy the Fox
1420.	**At the Eleventh Hour**	
1421.	**Up for the Jubilee**	
1422.	**Harry Wharton's Double**	The Stacey series
1423.	**Rivals of the Remove**	
1424.	**Harry Wharton's Enemy**	
1425.	**The Hero of the Hour**	
1426.	**Who Shall be Captain?**	
1427.	**Harry Wharton's Triumph**	
1428.	**The Black Sheep**	
1429.	**A Traitor to His Side**	
1430.	**A Dangerous Double**	
1431.	**Standing by Smithy**	
1432.	**Saved from the Sack**	
1433.	**Harry Wharton Wins Through**	
1434.	**Fish's Holiday Stunt**	Portercliffe Hall, Sussex
1435.	**The Mystery of Portercliffe Hall**	
1436.	**The Phantom of Portercliff**	
1437.	**The Greyfriars Gold Hunter**	
1438.	**The Man in the Mask**	
1439.	**On the Trail of Treasure**	
1440.	**Under False Colours**	Jim Warren
1441.	**The Spy of the Fifth**	
1442.	**Greyfriars Idiot No 1**	
1443.	**The Boy with a Borrowed Name**	
1444.	**Bunter Tells the Truth**	
1445.	**Saved By His Enemy**	

No.	Date	Title	Series
1446.		The Fifth-Former's Secret	
1447.		Guyed on the Fifth	
1448.		Football Foes	
1449.		Bunter Gets His Own Back	
1450.		Blackmail!	
1451.		Bunter Spills the Beans	
1452.		Smithy's Strange Adventure	Christmas at Polpelly
1453.		The Spectre of Polpelly	
1454.		The House of Mystery	
1455.		Galleon Gold	
1456.		Bunter's Bid for a Fortune	
1457.		The Boy Who Wouldn't Make Friends	Eric Wilmot
1458.		The Outsider	
1459.		The Form Master's Favourite	
1460.		The Remove's Recruit	
1461.		The Trail of Adventure	Harry Wharton and Co in Brazil
1462.	4 - 1 - 1936	Rolling Down to Rio	
1463.		The Wolf of Brazil	
1464.		Shadowed in South America	
1465.		The Vengeance of The Wolf	
1466.		The Greyfriars Diamond Diggers	
1467.		The Prisoner of Macaw Island	
1468.		The Millionaire Stowaway	
1469.		His Record Condemned Him	Home again, and Eric Wilmot
1470.		Not Wanted at Greyfriars	
1471.		His Gunman Guardian	Putnam van Duck
1472.		Gunplay at Greyfriars	

1473.	**Horace Coker's Dark Deed**	
1474.	**The Gangsters Swoop**	
1475.	**Ordered to Quit**	
1476.	**Bunter Beats the Gangsters**	
1477.	**The Vengeance of Bunter the Ventriloquist**	
1478.	**The Bogus Beak**	
1479.	**Billy Bunter's Burglar**	
1480.	**The Popper Court Tea Party**	
1481.	**Bunter the Lion Tamer**	Muscolini's Circus
1482.	**Billy Bunter's Bunk**	
1483.	**From School to Circus**	
1484.	**The Circus Schoolboy**	
1485.	**The Haunted Circus**	
1486.	**The Rascal of the Remove**	
1487.	**Not Wanted in the Circus**	
1488.	**The Signor's Secret**	
1489.	**The Hero of the Circus**	
1490.	**The Boy Who Knew Too Much**	
1491.	**Johnny Bull on the Run**	
1492.	**Schemers of Study No 7**	
1493.	**His Convict Cousin**	Loder's Convict cousin
1494.	**The Convict Who Came Back**	
1495.	**The Spy of the Sixth**	
1496.	**The Shadow of the Sack**	
1497.	**His Scapegrace Brother**	
1498.	**Harry Wharton's Amazing Rebellion**	
1499.	**The Secret of the Smugglers Cave**	Valentine Compton, the Schoolboy Smuggler

No.	Date	Title	Series
1500.		They Called Him a Funk	
1501.		The Schoolboy Smuggler	
1502.		Contraband	
1503.		The Boy With An Enemy	
1504.		The Way of the Transgressor	
1505.		Billy Bunter's Christmas Party	
1506.		The Cruise of the Firefly	
1507.	2 - 1 - 1937	The Man from the Sea	
1508.		The Ship of Secrets	
1509.		Mutiny on the Firefly	
1510.		Billy Bunter's Housewarming	
1511.		The Stay-In Strike at Greyfriars	The Tuckshop Rebellion
1512.		The No-Surrender Schoolboys	
1513.		Holding the Fort	
1514.		The Fighting Form	
1515.		The Prisoner of the Stronghold	
1516.		Coker the Kidnapper	
1517.		The Man With the Glaring Eyes	Highcliffe School in the Limelight
1518.		The Ananias of the Remove	Ponsonby and Co
1519.		Ponsonby Pulls the Strings	
1520.		Keeping Quelch Quiet	
1521.		The Heavy Hand	
1522.		Billy Bunter's Lucky Day	An Attempt on Mr Vernon Smith's life
1523.		The Shadowed Millionaire	
1524.		The Bounder's Peril	
1525.		The Trail in the Sand	
1526.		Billy Bunter's Coronation Party	

1527.	**Coker the Conqueror**	
1528.	**The Feud with Cliff House**	Harry Wharton & Co's Feud with Cliff House
1529.	**The Boy Who Wouldn't Split**	
1530.	**On the Track of the Trickster**	
1531.	**Bunter on the Spot**	Bunter gets £50 reward for capturing a crook
1532.	**Billy Bunter's Windfall**	
1533.	**The Bad Hat of the Remove**	Hazeldine in trouble with Bob Cherry shielding him
1534.	**Bob Cherry's Burden**	
1535.	**Barring Bob Cherry**	
1536.	**Spoofing the School**	Archie Popper
1537.	**The Boy Who Came Back**	
1538.	**The Invisible Schoolboy**	
1539.	**The Boy Behind the Scenes**	
1540.	**Wibley Wins Through**	
1541.	**The Sinister Doctor Sin**	At attempt on Wun Lung's life
1542.	**The House of Peril**	
1543.	**The Menace from the East**	
1544.	**The Greyfriars Crusoes**	
1545.	**The Boy Who Couldn't Run Straight**	Skip, the ex-pickpocket
1546.	**Coker Takes Control**	
1547.	**Coker's Big Idea**	
1548.	**Skip of the Remove**	
1549.	**The Outcast of the School**	
1550.	**Bad Lad Smithy**	
1551.	**The Big Bang at Greyfriars**	
1552.	**The Schoolboy Sleuth**	
1553.	**The Runaway Schoolboy**	

1554.		Skip's Lucky Break	
1555.		Bunter's Orders	
1556.		My Lord Bunter	My Lord Bunter
1557.		King of the Castle	
1558.		The Wraith of Raynham Castle	
1559.	1 - 1 - 1938	Lord Bunter's Bodyguard	
1560.		Bunter's Big Blunder	Single Story
1561.		Billy Bunter's Rich Relation	Arthur Carter
1562.		Bunter the Bragger	
1563.		Rivals for Riches	
1564.		Bunter's Big Bluff	
1565.		Getting His Own Back	
1566.		The Schemer of the Remove	
1567.		A Ventriloquist's Vengeance	
1568.		Billy Bunter's Dead Cert	
1569.		Carter Takes the Count	
1570.		Bunter Gets the Boot	
1571.		Billy Bunter's Twin	
1572.		Goodbye Greyfriars	Arthur Carter expelled for stealing
1573.		Bound for the Wild West	Harry Wharton and Co in Texas
1574.		On the Texas Trail	
1575.		Harry Wharton & Co in Texas	
1576.		The Schoolboy Range Riders	
1577.		Ructions on the Ranch	
1578.		A Prisoner in the Desert	
1579.		The Raid of the Kicking Cayuse Ranch	Rio Kid
1580.		The Man with the Hidden Face	

1581.	The Trail Thief's Secret	
1582.	The Trail Thief's Last Ride	
1583.	Bunter the Hypnotist	
1584.	Walker on the Warpath	
1585.	Five in a Fix	The Co against Ponsonby and Loder
1586.	Up For the Sack	
1587.	Punishing Ponsonby	
1588.	Loder's Unlucky Day	Single Story
1589.	South Seas Adventure	Harry Wharton & Co in the South Seas with
1590.	The Outlaw of Kalua	Mauleverer – they meet Ken King of the Islands
1591.	The Schoolboy Crusoes	
1592.	The Beachcomber's Secret	
1593.	The Scuttled Schooner	
1594.	Adrift in the Pacific	
1595.	Big Chief Bunter	
1596.	The Castaways of Cannibal Island	
1597.	The Man Behind the Scenes	
1598.	Saved By a Foe	
1599.	The Boy Who Wouldn't be Tamed	Gilbert Tracy
1600.	The Rat of the Remove	
1601.	The Runaway	
1602.	Tricky Tracy	
1603.	The Mystery of Mr Quelch	
1604.	He Let The Side Down	
1605.	Saved By His Enemy	
1606.	Tracy Takes the Blame	
1607.	The Mysterious Night Raider	

1608.	**Tracking Down Tracy**	
1609.	**Harry Wharton's Christmas Guest**	Christmas at Wharton Lodge
1610.	**The Mystery of Wharton Lodge**	
1611.	**A Baffling Quest**	
1612. 7 - 1 - 1939	**Spotting the Secret**	
1613.	**The Sportsman of the Fourth**	
1614.	**Saving Bunter's Bacon**	
1615.	**Loker Looks for Trouble**	Croker the Old Boy - boot repairer late of the
1616.	**The Mystery Man of Greyfriars**	Sixth who was expelled for stealing
1617.	**The Hoaxing of Hacker**	
1618.	**Sexton Blake Minor**	
1619.	**Duffer or Detective?**	
1620.	**The Old Boy's Vengeance**	
1621.	**Who Sacked Hacker?**	
1622.	**Harry Wharton's Secret**	
1623	**Guilty Gold**	
1624.	**The Clue of the Purple Footprints**	
1625.	**Drake Gets His Man**	
1626.	**Billy Bunter's Easter Trip**	Easter on Blackrock Island
1627.	**The Mystery of Blackrock Island**	
1628.	**The Kidnapped Millionaire**	
1629.	**The Secret of the Sea Cave**	
1630.	**Fools' Luck**	
1631.	**The Mystery of Vernon-Smith**	Bertie Vernon
1632.	**The Bounder's Double**	
1633.	**The Perfect Alibi**	
1634.	**The Kidnapped Cricketer**	

1635.	**Rough on His Rival**	
1636.	**The Rebel of the Remove**	
1637.	**The Prisoner of the Turrett**	
1638.	**A Double in Trouble**	
1639.	**The Greyfriars Imposter**	
1640.	**The House of Dark Secrets**	
1641.	**The Plotter**	
1642.	**The Plot that Failed**	
1643.	**The Greyfriars Stowaway**	Harry Wharton & Co on the Thames
1644.	**Ructions on the River**	The Secret of the Water Lily
1645.	**Six Boys in a Boat**	
1646.	**Greyfriars to the Rescue**	
1647.	**Coker Takes Command**	
1648.	**Mystery on the Thames**	
1649.	**Bunter on the Spot**	
1650.	**The Secret of the Water Lily**	
1651.	**Condemned Without Evidence**	Smithy versus Mr Quelch and Wingate
1652.	**Grunter of Greyhurst**	
1653.	**The Bounder's Dupe**	
1654.	**The Black Prince of Greyfriars**	
1655.	**The Tuck Hoarder**	
1656.	**Run Out of Greyfriars**	Coker sacked
1657.	**The Remove Detectives**	
1658.	**The Wanderer's Return**	
1659.	**Billy Bunter's Bargain**	
1660.	**The Man in the Mask**	Mr Lamb
1661.	**The Phantom of the Moat House**	

1662.		**The Man of Mystery**	
1663.		**The Boy from Baker Street**	
1664.	**6 - 1 - 1940**	**The Hooded Man**	
1665.		**Smithy's Secret Weapon**	
1666.		**The Bounder on the Trail**	
1667.		**Six on the Warpath**	
1668.		**The Japer of Greyfriars**	
1669.		**The Secret of the Dugout**	
1670.		**The Thief of the Night**	
1671.		**A Black-Out Blunder**	
1672.		**The Eleventh Hour**	
1673.		**Vernon Smith's Last Fling**	
1674.		**Bounder and Sticker**	
1675.		**The Bounder's Triumph**	
1676.		**Sir William's Double**	The Mystery of Eastcliffe Lodge
1677.		**The Mystery Man of Eastcliffe Lodge**	
1678.		**The Unseen Enemy**	
1679.		**Billy Bunter's Hair Raid**	
1680.		**The Man from Germany**	
1681.		**The Spy of the Gestapo**	
1682.		**The Nazi Spy's Secret**	
	18 - 5 - 1940		
1683.		**The Shadow of the Sack**	New series with Harry Wharton in trouble

1683 issues featuring Greyfriars School all published under the pen name of *Frank Richards.*

Stories written but not published (manuscripts now lost)

1684. The Battle of the Beaks
1685. Bandy Bunter ** (The Meddler)
1686. What Happened to Hacker?
1687. The Hidden Hand

** editorial change of title.

ss Denotes that the story is a substitute and not written by Charles Hamilton (Frank Richards). It should be emphasised that some of these stories, especially during J.N. Pentelow's editorship, had more than one author writing them. The original writer as shown by official stock-book records are given in these cases.

This catalogue was compiled by our consulting expert on Magnet affairs – W.O.G. Lofts; who holds official records gleaned from Amalgamated Press files, and information supplied by C.M. Down, Magnet editor. Any queries regarding data included in this catalogue should be addressed to him, c/o the Publishers.

THE MAGNET

Published by Amalgamated Press Limited
1,683 issues. 15th February, 1908 to 18th May, 1940

Price	½d	1 - 105 (except 104, which was 1d)
Price	1d	106 - 528
Price	1½d	529 - 769
Price	2d	770 - 1,683

1 - 396	Red
397 - 769	Blue and White
770 - 1552	Orange/Yellow and Blue
1553 - 1683	Salmon

CONTROLLING EDITORS

1908 - 1911	Percy Griffith (presumed deceased)
1911 - 1916	Herbert Allan Hinton
1916 - 1919	(Nos 421 to 579) John Nix Pentelow (d 1931)
1919 - 1921	Herbert Allan Hinton (d. 1945)
1921 - 1940	Charles Maurice Down

ALL THE RECORDED AUTHORS OF 'SUBSTITUTE STORIES'

Writers, other than Charles Hamilton, who produced
Magnet stories published under the pen-name of
'Frank Richards'.

S. E. Austin. (died 1950's) Wrote a considerable number of substitute stories for both the Magnet and the Gem, chiefly the latter, from 1919 to the mid-30's. Contributed also to: Boys' Herald, Boys' Realm, Boys Friend Weekly, Chums, Nelson Lee Library, Lloyds Sports Library, Lloyds School Yarns, and British Boy.

Robert J. Barnard. With his father (Alfred J. Barnard) and his brother (Richard Innes Barnard) wrote for both the Magnet and the Gem. Some difficulty must exist in reliably attributing particular stories to him rather than to his brother, since both signed themselves 'R. Barnard'.

S. Barrie. Nothing is known for certain about this writer. But there is evidence for believing that the name was a pseudonym concealing the identity of one of the senior editors of The Amalgamated Press.

Edwy Searles Brooks (1889–1965). Wrote extensively for the Nelson Lee Library and for the Union Jack (Sexton Blake stories) as well as for a host of other Amalgamated Press and Thomson boys' papers. Produced substitute stories for the Gem as well as for the Magnet, and was also known in the hard-cover and paperback thriller field as 'Norman Conquest' and 'Victor Gunn'.

William Leslie Catchpole. A winner of Greyfriars Story Competition, 1915. One-time film writer, and recently retired insurance executive. Probable author of all small contributions to the Magnet and the Gem from 1926 to 1940. Also contributed to The Holiday Annual, Ranger and Union Jack.

F. G. Cook. (1900–   ). Was junior sub-editor on Chums and contributed occasional stories. First Magnet story (591) was followed by about thirty others, and probably twice this number in the Gem. From 1927 to 1933, contributed regularly to The Boys' Magazine and a little-known boys' paper called Toby.

A. W. Davis. Wrote only two substitute stories (991 and 993) and was believed to be in the greengrocery business.

C. M. Down. Magnet editor. q.v.

Hedley Percival Angelo O'Mant (1899–1955). Of Irish-Italian parentage. First job was with Aldine Publications, but soon transferred to staff of Amalgamated Press. Later became Chief Sub-Editor on the Magnet. After service in the First World War edited many Amalgamated Press boys' papers: Nelson Lee, Ranger, and Pilot, and wrote extensively under many pen-names – mainly flying stories (he served in the R.A.F. in both World Wars).

John Nix Pentelow. Magnet editor. **q.v.**

William Ernest Pike. Joined the staff of Amalgamated Press in 1915 as sub-editor on the Magnet. Wrote one substitute story for the Magnet and one of Rookwood for the Boys' Friend, of which he was the last editor.

L. E. Ransome. Winner of Greyfriars Story competition, 1915. Joined the staff of Amalgamated Press in 1916 and worked on the Companion Papers and Boys' Friend. Went free-lance in 1921, and since that time has contributed thousands of stories to both boys' and girls' papers, under many non-de-plumes.

George Richmond Samways (1895–). On the staff of Amalgamated Press from before the First World War to 1921. Wrote substitute stories for the Gem as well as for the Magnet, and also originated the Greyfriars Herald and St. Jim's Gazette as well as creating the humorous stories of Dr. Birchemal of St. Sam's (adapted from the first half of Samways' own name). Free-lanced after 1921 and in 1929 became a professional competition solutionist, winning many big prizes for himself and his clients in national competitions.

S. Rossiter Shepherd. Theatre and holiday expert. Wrote substitute stories for the Magnet in the 1921–1925 period. Was editor of Picturegoer, and also crime reporter on the Daily Express and Features Editor and film critic of The People.

Noel Wood-Smith (died 1955). On the staff of Companion Papers, and during the 1920's was chief sub-editor and deputy to C. M. Down on the Magnet, when he wrote some substitute Greyfriars stories. Also wrote Sexton Blake stories for the Union Jack. He was a clever inventor and had many ideas accepted by leading business firms.

H. W. Twyman. (1898–). Joined the Amalgamated Press as a proof reader on the Magnet and the Gem in 1914, and soon afterwards was appointed Chief Sub-Editor on Chuckles. After war service was made editor of the Detective Library and, later, Nugget Weekly. In 1921 took over the editorship of Union Jack. Still later was editor of Detective Weekly. He left the Amalgamated Press before the Second World War and joined the staff of the Sunday Pictorial. In 1941 he joined the Ministry of Information, and in 1945 worked on Man of the World and, in 1946, on Commonwealth Review.

M. F. Duffy. (1906–). Trade journalist and author of the last substitute story to appear in the Magnet (1220) in 1931. The remaining Magnet stories (1221 to 1683) were all written by Charles Hamilton.

William Gibbons. (1900–). Believed to be the son of William Gibbons, the famous comedian. Winner of the Greyfriars Story competition. Worked on the staff of the Amalgamated Press (Boys' Friend Library) and also wrote numerous stories for The Champion/Triumph group. Also wrote girls' stories under the pseudonym of 'Helen Gibbons'.

Julius Herman (1894–1955). Born South Africa. A school-teacher. Contributed also to the Gem, The Greyfriars Herald and the Holiday Annual. A photograph of him appeared in the Nelson Lee Library in the April 29th, 1929 issue.

Herbert Allan Hinton. (Magnet editor) **q.v.**

H. Clarke Hook. Son of the famous writer, S. Clarke Hook, who created Jack, Sam and Pete for The Marvel. Wrote substitute stories in the Gem as well as the Magnet, and also contributed to Pluck and to Chums as 'Ross Harvey'. Believed to have also written a good many girls' and adult stories.

William Edward Stanton Hope (1889–1961). Took job at Amalgamated Press in 1904 as an office boy. Later was on the Companion Papers staff and later still took over as editor of Chuckles. Became free-lance writer after the First World War and wrote 'Herlock Sholmes', parodies in The Greyfriars Herald, and Sexton Blake stories, amongst many others. Published his autobiography, 'Rolling Round the World for Fun' in 1925. Founded the 'Stanton Hope College of Journalism' in Sydney, Australia, after World War II.

Alec M. Kemp. On the staff of Amalgamated Press, and wrote for Boys' Friend Weekly, Film Fun, Kinema Comic, Fun and Fiction, Surprise, Butterfly, Favourite Comic and Merry & Bright, as well as writing substitute stories for the Magnet. Had a style remarkably similar to Edwy Searles Brooks.

Reginald S. Kirkham. Was on the staff of the Amalgamated Press for a short time before going free-lance in 1920. Wrote substitute stories for the Gem as well as for the Magnet, and took over the Cliff House stories from Charles Hamilton in School Friend. Also contributed to Boys' Friend Weekly and Boys' Journal.

Kenneth E. Newman. Editor and author of the short-lived 'School Yarn Magazine' which appeared in 1947 – based on 'Rippingham School' which Newman had created for a BBC series in 1936. Wrote substitute stories featuring St Jim's and Rookwood as well as Greyfriars.

INDEX OF MAGNET STORIES

Title	Year	No.
BARRED BY HIS FORM	(1933)	1320
BARRED BY HIS PEOPLE	(1911)	177
BARRED BY THE FAGS	(1913)	269
BARRING BOB CHERRY	(1937)	1535
BARRING OF BOLSOVER, THE	(1925)	890
BARRING OF BULSTRODE, THE	(1909)	71
BARRING OF BUNTER, THE	(1924)	848
BARRING OUT AT GREYFRIARS, THE	(1917)	504
BEACHCOMBER'S SECRET, THE	(1938)	1592
BE CAREFUL, CHRISTOPHER	(1928)	1079
BEGGAR OF SHANTUNG, THE	(1930)	1184
BESSIE VERSUS BILLY	(1919)	595
BID FOR THE CAPTAINCY, A	(1920)	654
BIG BANG AT GREYFRIARS, THE	(1937)	1551
BIG CHIEF BUNTER	(1938)	1595
BILLIONAIRING WITH BUNTER	(1934)	1385
BILLY BUNTER - EDITOR	(1909)	76
BILLY BUNTER, FILMSTAR	(1922)	736
BILLY BUNTER, HYPNOTIST	(1908)	30
BILLY BUNTER LTD.	(1910)	130
BILLY BUNTER ON THE FILMS	(1929)	1099
BILLY BUNTER'S BAD LUCK	(1932)	1277
BILLY BUNTER'S BANK HOLIDAY	(1919)	592
BILLY BUNTER'S BANKNOTE	(1932)	1274
BILLY BUNTER'S BARGAIN	(1931)	1221
BILLY BUNTER'S BARGAIN	(1932)	1281
BILLY BUNTER'S BARGAIN	(1939)	1659
BILLY BUNTER'S BARGAINS	(1933)	1306
BILLY BUNTER'S BIG BARGAIN	(1922)	729
BILLY BUNTER'S BIRTHRIGHT	(1918)	538
BILLY BUNTER'S BLUFF	(1930)	1147
BILLY BUNTER'S BLUNDER	(1929)	1109
BILLY BUNTER'S BOAT RACE PARTY	(1923)	789
BILLY BUNTER'S BOLT	(1916)	449
BILLY BUNTER'S BOLT	(1925)	916
BILLY BUNTER'S BOOKMAKER	(1928)	1068
BILLY BUNTER'S BRAINWAVE	(1925)	910
BILLY BUNTER'S BUNK	(1931)	1206
BILLY BUNTER'S BUNK	(1936)	1482
BILLY BUNTER'S BURGLAR	(1936)	1479
BILLY BUNTER'S CAMPAIGN	(1924)	877
BILLY BUNTER'S CERT	(1932)	1249
BILLY BUNTER'S CHRISTMAS	(1929)	1140
BILLY BUNTER'S CHRISTMAS	(1930)	1191
BILLY BUNTER'S CHRISTMAS DREAM	(1909)	95
BILLY BUNTER'S CHRISTMAS PARTY	(1936)	1505
BILLY BUNTER'S CIRCUS	(1928)	1071
BILLY BUNTER'S COMEBACK	(1930)	1151
BILLY BUNTER'S CONVICT	(1928)	1039
BILLY BUNTER'S CORONATION PARTY	(1937)	1526

BILLY BUNTER'S DEAD CERT	(1938)	1568
BILLY BUNTER'S EASTER CRUISE	(1933)	1312
BILLY BUNTER'S EASTER TRIP	(1939)	1626
BILLY BUNTER'S HAIR RAID	(1940)	1679
BILLY BUNTER'S HAT TRICK	(1931)	1226
BILLY BUNTER'S HAT TRICK	(1933)	1326
BILLY BUNTER'S HOUSEWARMING	(1909)	54
BILLY BUNTER'S HOUSEWARMING	(1937)	1510
BILLY BUNTER'S KICKOFF	(1910)	136
BILLY BUNTER'S LEGACY	(1926)	941
BILLY BUNTER'S LUCK	(1921)	701
BILLY BUNTER'S LUCK	(1928)	1069
BILLY BUNTER'S LUCKY DAY	(1937)	1522
BILLY BUNTER'S MASTERSTROKE	(1925)	912
BILLY BUNTER'S MINOR	(1910)	144
BILLY BUNTER'S RAID	(1908)	40
BILLY BUNTER'S REFORMATION	(1916)	460
BILLY BUNTER'S RESOLUTION	(1910)	99
BILLY BUNTER'S RICH RELATION	(1938)	1561
BILLY BUNTER'S SMUGGLERS	(1921)	677
BILLY BUNTER'S SPECULATION	(1920)	643
BILLY BUNTER'S TRIALS	(1910)	114
BILLY BUNTER'S TWIN	(1938)	1571
BILLY BUNTER'S UNCLE	(1914)	358
BILLY BUNTER'S VENGEANCE	(1932)	1265
BILLY BUNTER'S VOTE	(1910)	116
BILLY BUNTER'S WEMBLEY PARTY	(1924)	870
BILLY BUNTER'S WHEEZE	(1919)	570
BILLY BUNTER'S WINDFALL	(1909)	87
BILLY BUNTER'S WINDFALL	(1937)	1532
BILLY'S BOOM	(1908)	11
BILLY'S COMPETITION	(1908)	14
BILLY'S TREAT	(1908)	20
BIRD OF PASSAGE, A	(1918)	527
BITER BIT, THE	(1913)	302
BLACK FOOTBALLERS, THE	(1914)	354
BLACK MAGIC	(1928)	1050
BLACK MAGIC	(1933)	1305
BLACKMAIL	(1929)	1133
BLACKMAIL !	(1935)	1450
BLACK PETER'S TREASURE	(1927)	1025
BLACK MAN AT GREYFRIARS, THE	(1922)	774
BLACK-OUT BLUNDER, A	(1940)	1671
BLACK PRINCE OF GREYFRIARS, THE	(1939)	1654
BLACK SHEEP, THE	(1935)	1428
BLACK SHEEP OF HIGHCLIFFE, THE	(1919)	576
BLACK SHEEP OF THE SIXTH, THE	(1929)	1114
BLINDNESS OF BUNTER, THE	(1920)	634
BLUFFING THE BEAK	(1931)	1222
BLUNDELL'S PRIZE	(1914)	317

BOUNDER'S WIN, THE	(1927)	1007
BOUND FOR AFRICA	(1922)	769
BOUND FOR AFRICA	(1924)	864
BOUND FOR AMERICA	(1929)	1093
BOUND FOR BHANIPUR	(1926)	966
BOUND FOR THE WILD WEST	(1938)	1573
BOWLING OUT BUNTER	(1926)	934
BOXING BEAK, THE	(1933)	1321
BOY BEHIND THE SCENES, THE	(1937)	1539
BOY FROM BAKER STREET, THE	(1939)	1663
BOY FROM SOUTH AFRICA, THE	(1916)	432
BOY FROM THE EAST, THE	(1928)	1059
BOY FROM THE FARM, THE	(1914)	329
BOY FROM THE UNDERWORLD, THE	(1932)	1297
BOY HEADMASTER, THE	(1928)	1048
BOY SCOUTS FROM THE 'FADERLAND'	(1909)	80
BOY'S CROSSROADS, A	(1925)	909
BOY WHO CAME BACK, THE	(1937)	1537
BOY WHO COULDN'T RUN STRAIGHT, THE	(1937)	1545
BOY WHO FOUND HIS FATHER, THE	(1927)	1004
BOY WHO KNEW TOO MUCH, THE	(1931)	1217
BOY WHO KNEW TOO MUCH, THE	(1936)	1490
BOY WHO WOULDN'T BE TAMED, THE	(1938)	1599
BOY WHO WOULDN'T MAKE FRIENDS, THE	(1935)	1457
BOY WHO WOULDN'T SPLIT, THE	(1937)	1529
BOY WITH A BAD NAME, THE	(1923)	794
BOY WITH A BORROWED NAME, THE	(1935)	1443
BOY WITH A GUILTY SECRET, THE	(1933)	1300
BOY WITH AN ENEMY, THE	(1936)	1503
BOY WITH A PAST, THE	(1928)	1080
BOY WITHOUT A FRIEND, THE	(1929)	1126
BOY WITHOUT A NAME, THE	(1931)	1195
BRAVO,BULSTRODE !	(1922)	754
BRAVO,BUNTER !	(1919)	574
BRAVO,BUNTER !	(1927)	1016
BRAVO,THE BOUNDER !	(1913)	294
BROKEN BOND, THE	(1918)	554
BROTHER AND PREFECT	(1925)	923
BROTHERHOOD OF JUSTICE, THE	(1934)	1397
BROTHER'S SACRIFICE, A	(1931)	1243
BRUISER OF THE REMOVE, THE	(1927)	986
BUCK UP, BUNTER	(1925)	900
BULLY OF GREYFRIARS, THE	(1909)	69
BULLY'S BROTHER, THE	(1911)	178
BULLY'S CHANCE, THE	(1911)	195
BULLY'S REMORSE, THE	(1911)	169
BULSTRODE ON THE WARPATH	(1911)	176
BUNKING OF BILLY BUNTER, THE	(1934)	1374
BUNKING OF BUNTER, THE	(1924)	876
BUNTER BEATS THE GANGSTERS	(1936)	1476

Title	Year	No.
BUNTER - BIG GAME HUNTER	(1929)	1091
BUNTER CAUGHT	(1925)	917
BUNTER COMES TO STAY	(1928)	1076
BUNTER COMES TO STAY	(1929)	1141
BUNTER COURT ELEVEN, THE	(1925)	914
BUNTER GETS HIS OWN BACK	(1935)	1449
BUNTER GETS THE BOOT	(1938)	1570
BUNTER ON THE BOARDS	(1919)	619
BUNTER ON THE SPOT	(1937)	1531
BUNTER ON THE SPOT	(1939)	1649
BUNTER OF BUNTER COURT	(1925)	911
BUNTER'S £100 BOATER	(1933)	1325
BUNTER SPILLS THE BEANS	(1935)	1451
BUNTER TELLS THE TRUTH	(1935)	1444
BUNTER'S AMAZING ADVENTURE	(1929)	1097
BUNTER'S ANTI-TUCK CAMPAIGN	(1915)	401
BUNTER'S AUCTION	(1919)	590
BUNTER'S AUNT SALLY	(1919)	599
BUNTER'S BABY	(1920)	652
BUNTER'S BANK NOTES	(1915)	371
BUNTER'S BARRING OUT	(1923)	802
BUNTER'S BARRING-IN	(1926)	957
BUNTER'S BID FOR A FORTUNE	(1935)	1456
BUNTER'S BIG BLUFF	(1928)	1072
BUNTER'S BIG BLUFF	(1933)	1316
BUNTER'S BIG BLUFF	(1938)	1564
BUNTER'S BIG BLUNDER	(1938)	1560
BUNTER'S BIG BROTHER	(1917)	469
BUNTER'S BIKE	(1928)	1056
BUNTER'S BLACK CHUM	(1914)	312
BUNTER'S BLUFF	(1920)	651
BUNTER'S BODYGUARD	(1928)	1073
BUNTER'S BOLT	(1922)	737
BUNTER'S BRAINSTORM	(1927)	996
BUNTER'S BUST-UP	(1910)	148
BUNTER'S CHRISTMAS PORTRAIT	(1919)	620
BUNTER'S CHRISTMAS PRESENT	(1927)	1036
BUNTERS' CONSPIRACY, THE	(1922)	732
BUNTER'S LATEST	(1918)	526
BUNTER'S LATEST	(1923)	787
BUNTER'S LAWSUIT	(1922)	767
BUNTER'S NIGHT OUT	(1932)	1247
BUNTER'S ORDERS	(1937)	1555
BUNTER'S PICNIC	(1921)	693
BUNTER'S POOR RELATIONS	(1924)	836
BUNTER'S PRIZE ESSAY	(1928)	1054
BUNTER'S RAFFLE	(1922)	753
BUNTER'S TREASURE TROVE	(1926)	955
BUNTER'S TYPING AGENCY	(1919)	603
BUNTER'S VENGEANCE	(1909)	51

BUNTER'S VERY LATEST	(1921)	715
BUNTER THE BAD LAD	(1927)	1014
BUNTER THE BANDIT	(1921)	699
BUNTER THE BANDIT	(1929)	1137
BUNTER THE BANKRUPT	(1920)	639
BUNTER THE BARD	(1921)	711
BUNTER THE BENEVOLENT	(1927)	1037
BUNTER THE BILLIONAIRE	(1934)	1383
BUNTER THE BLADE	(1915)	366
BUNTER THE BOLD	(1927)	1005
BUNTER THE BOLSHEVIK	(1919)	593
BUNTER THE BOSS	(1928)	1070
BUNTER THE BOXER	(1909)	81
BUNTER THE BRAGGER	(1938)	1562
BUNTER THE BULLY	(1909)	83
BUNTER THE BULLY	(1933)	1348
BUNTER THE CAVALIER	(1925)	897
BUNTER THE CROOK	(1922)	748
BUNTER THE DETECTIVE	(1909)	92
BUNTER THE DODGER	(1934)	1376
BUNTER THE FARMER	(1920)	644
BUNTER THE FOOTBALLER	(1933)	1303
BUNTER THE HUNTER	(1923)	810
BUNTER THE HYPNOTIST	(1938)	1583
BUNTER THE INK SPLASHER	(1930)	1160
BUNTER THE LION TAMER	(1936)	1481
BUNTER THE MASHER	(1915)	410
BUNTER THE MASHER	(1934)	1351
BUNTER THE PRIZE HUNTER	(1930)	1159
BUNTER THE PRIZEWINNER	(1913)	292
BUNTER THE PROPHET	(1925)	892
BUNTER THE PUNTER	(1918)	568
BUNTER THE STOWAWAY	(1927)	1020
BUNTER THE SWOT	(1921)	684
BUNTER THE VENTRILOQUIST	(1933)	1328
BUNTER THE VENTRILOQUIST	(1934)	1369
BUNTER TO THE RESCUE	(1918)	532
BY LUCK AND PLUCK	(1928)	1061
BY ORDER OF THE FORM	(1911)	203
BY SHEER GRIT	(1911)	194
BY WINGATE'S AID	(1921)	681
CAD'S TRIAL, THE	(1910)	120
CALL OF THE CIRCUS, THE	(1930)	1168
CALL OF THE DESERT, THE	(1924)	866
CALL OF THE RING, THE	(1927)	990
CALLED TO THE COLOURS	(1916)	436
CALL FROM THE AIR, THE	(1922)	775
CAPPED FOR GREYFRIARS	(1924)	849
CAPTAIN AND TYRANT	(1925)	928
CAPTAIN BOB CHERRY	(1910)	135

DUFFER OR DETECTIVE	(1939)	1619
DUFFER'S DOUBLE, THE	(1912)	205
DUFFER'S RETURN, THE	(1911)	201
DUPING THE DUFFER	(1920)	669
EASY TERMS	(1914)	320
ELEVENTH HOUR, THE	(1940)	1672
END OF THE SIXTH, THE	(1910)	107
EXILED FROM SCHOOL	(1920)	623
EXPELLED !	(1908)	46
EYE OF OSIRIS, THE	(1932)	1284
FACING THE MUSIC	(1919)	614
FACING THE MUSIC	(1935)	1417
FACING THE WORLD	(1925)	932
FACTORY REBELS, THE	(1914)	313
FAGGING FOR COKER	(1914)	355
FAITHFUL TO HIS FRIEND	(1921)	724
FALLEN FORTUNES	(1918)	556
FALL OF ALGERNON, THE	(1922)	752
FALL OF THE BOUNDER, THE	(1917)	487
FALL OF THE FIFTH, THE	(1915)	374
FALSE EVIDENCE	(1916)	427
FALSE FORM MASTER, THE	(1913)	285
FALSE HERO, A	(1920)	657
FAMOUS FOUR, THE	(1908)	21
FAREWELL TO THE FILMS	(1929)	1107
FED UP WITH GREYFRIARS	(1927)	995
FELLOW WHO FUNKED, THE	(1917)	470
FELLOW WHO WON, THE	(1915)	394
FELLOW WHO WOULDN'T BE CANED, THE	(1928)	1042
FEUD WITH CLIFF HOUSE, THE	(1925)	902
FEUD WITH CLIFF HOUSE, THE	(1937)	1528
FEUD WITH FRIARDALE, THE	(1920)	635
FEUD WITH THE FOURTH, A	(1926)	943
'FIFTH' AT GREYFRIARS, THE	(1909)	91
FIFTH FORM MYSTERY, THE	(1935)	1411
FIFTH-FORMER'S SECRET, THE	(1935)	1446
FIFTY POUNDS REWARD	(1915)	383
FIGHT FOR THE CAPTAINCY, A	(1912)	214
FIGHT FOR THE CUP, THE	(1915)	362
FIGHTING FIFTH, THE	(1918)	529
FIGHTING FORM, THE	(1937)	1514
FIGHTING TO THE FINISH	(1916)	435
FILMSTAR'S FEUD, THE	(1929)	1102
FILMSTAR'S VENGEANCE, A	(1929)	1105
'FIRST' AT GREYFRIARS, THE	(1910)	112
FIRST ELEVEN, THE	(1910)	121
FISH'S FAG AGENCY	(1913)	257
FISH'S HOLIDAY STUNT	(1935)	1434
FISHY'S BURGLAR HUNT	(1927)	1006
FISHY'S FEARFUL FIX	(1934)	1381

FISHY'S FRIENDLY SOCIETY	(1923)	815
FISHY'S HAIR-RAISING STUNT	(1925)	920
FISHY'S LATEST	(1916)	454
FISHY'S TRAVEL AGENCY	(1927)	993
FISHY'S TREASURE	(1924)	841
FISHY THE FOOTBALLER	(1922)	764
FIVE IN A FIX	(1938)	1585
FLAP'S BROTHER	(1917)	515
FLOORING FISHY	(1916)	420
FOE FROM AFRICA, THE	(1924)	863
FOE FROM THE SKY, THE	(1930)	1177
FOES OF THE FOURTH	(1912)	220
FOES OF THE REMOVE	(1919)	586
FOES OF THE REMOVE	(1931)	1240
FOES OF THE SAHARA	(1924)	867
FOES OF THE SIXTH	(1916)	417
FOES OF THE SIXTH	(1931)	1212
FOILING THE FOE	(1914)	350
FOOL OF THE FIFTH, THE	(1930)	1154
FOOL OF THE SCHOOL, THE	(1932)	1262
FOOLED ON THE FIRST	(1935)	1416
FOOLED ON THE FIFTH	(1934)	1395
FOOL'S LUCK	(1929)	1134
FOOL'S LUCK	(1935)	1407
FOOL'S LUCK	(1939)	1630
FOOTBALL HEROES	(1911)	192
FOOTBALLER'S FEUD, THE	(1922)	727
FOOTBALLER'S FOE, THE	(1922)	765
FOOTBALL FOES	(1935)	1448
FOOTPRINT IN THE SAND, THE	(1927)	992
FOR ANOTHER'S SAKE	(1926)	954
FOR ANOTHER'S SINS	(1919)	575
FORBIDDEN CHUM, A	(1912)	219
FORBIDDEN MATCH, THE	(1916)	430
FOR D'ARCY'S SAKE	(1916)	450
FOR HIS FATHER'S NAME	(1922)	747
FOR HIS MOTHER'S SAKE	(1912)	245
FORM MASTER AND ROGUE	(1934)	1364
FORM MASTER'S DISGRACE, THE	(1921)	680
FORM MASTER'S FATE, A	(1922)	734
FORM MASTER'S FAVOURITE, THE	(1930)	1143
FORM MASTER'S FAVOURITE, THE	(1935)	1459
FORM MASTER'S FEUD, THE	(1928)	1086
FORM MASTER'S FOE, THE	(1928)	1041
FORM MASTER'S SECRET, THE	(1912)	238
FORM MASTER'S SECRET, THE	(1934)	1363
FOR THE HONOUR OF GREYFRIARS	(1928)	1057
FOR THE HONOUR OF HIS CHUM	(1911)	196
FORTUNE AT STAKE, A	(1928)	1067
FORWARD FISH	(1911)	153

Title	Year	No.
GREAT FIFTH AT GREYFRIARS, THE	(1927)	1029
GREAT POSTAL ORDER MYSTERY, THE	(1925)	891
GREYFRIARS ARAB, THE	(1924)	862
GREYFRIARS ATHLETES, THE	(1910)	103
GREYFRIARS BARRING OUT, THE	(1922)	745
GREYFRIARS BUNFIGHT, THE	(1909)	77
GREYFRIARS CAMP, THE	(1909)	74
GREYFRIARS CARAVAN, THE	(1909)	73
GREYFRIARS CARAVANNERS, THE	(1921)	704
GREYFRIARS CARAVANNERS ABROAD	(1921)	709
GREYFRIARS CASTAWAYS, THE	(1927)	1026
GREYFRIARS CHALLENGE, THE	(1908)	19
GREYFRIARS CHINEE, THE	(1908)	37
GREYFRIARS CHRISTMAS PARTY, THE	(1917)	513
GREYFRIARS CHUMS AFLOAT, THE	(1933)	1313
GREYFRIARS CHUMS IN CHICAGO	(1929)	1095
GREYFRIARS CHUMS IN CHINA	(1930)	1182
GREYFRIARS CLOWN	(1911)	164
GREYFRIARS CONJURER, THE	(1908)	29
GREYFRIARS CRACKSMAN, THE	(1930)	1150
GREYFRIARS CRICKETERS, THE	(1909)	60
GREYFRIARS CRUSADERS, THE	(1912)	249
GREYFRIARS CRUSOES, THE	(1937)	1544
GREYFRIARS DAY BOARDER, THE	(1923)	801
GREYFRIARS DETECTIVES, THE	(1919)	609
GREYFRIARS DIAMOND DIGGERS, THE	(1936)	1466
GREYFRAIRS EXILE, THE	(1922)	740
GREYFRIARS FIFTEEN, THE	(1910)	104
GREYFRIARS FILM FANS	(1925)	921
GREYFRIARS FLIGHT, THE	(1910)	111
GREYFRIARS FLYING CORPS, THE	(1917)	476
GREYFRIARS FLOOD, THE	(1924)	833
GREYFRIARS GARDENERS, THE	(1912)	227
GREYFRIARS GLIDING COMPETITION,THE	(1923)	824
GREYFRIARS GOLDDIGGERS, THE	(1913)	299
GREYFRIARS GOLD HUNTER, THE	(1935)	1437
GREYFRIARS GUY, THE	(1933)	1342
GREYFRIARS HERALD, THE	(1913)	296
GREYFRIARS HERCULES, THE	(1933)	1346
GREYFRIARS HIKERS, THE	(1933)	1332
GREYFRIARS HYPNOTIST, THE	(1911)	157
GREYFRIARS IDIOT NO. 1	(1935)	1442
GREYFRIARS IMPOSTER, THE	(1939)	1639
GREYFRIARS INQUISITION, THE	(1917)	503
GREYFRIARS INSURANCE COMPANY, THE	(1912)	242
GREYFRIARS MINSTRELS, THE	(1920)	645
GREYFRIARS NEWSPAPER, THE	(1924)	831
GREYFRIARS ORGANISER, THE	(1917)	498
GREYFRIARS PANTOMIME, THE	(1913)	256
GREYFRIARS PHOTOGRAPHER, THE	(1909)	72

GREYFRIARS PICNIC	(1909)	63
GREYFRIARS PLOT, THE	(1910)	106
GREYFRIARS PRETENDER, THE	(1931)	1215
GREYFRIARS REBELLION, THE	(1930)	1171
GREYFRIARS RIOT, THE	(1908)	23
GREYFRIARS SAILORS, THE	(1909)	53
GREYFRIARS SKATERS, THE	(1909)	96
GREYFRIARS SLEEPWALKER, THE	(1908)	26
GREYFRIARS SPY-HUNTERS, THE	(1914)	348
GREYFRIARS STORMTROOPERS, THE	(1934)	1392
GREYFRIARS STOWAWAY	(1939)	1643
GREYFRIARS STRONG MAN, THE	(1933)	1344
GREYFRAIRS SWEEPSTAKE, THE	(1909)	97
GREYFRIARS SWIMMING SPORTS, THE	(1919)	594
GREYFRIARS TO THE RESCUE	(1939)	1646
GREYFRIARS TOURISTS, THE	(1919)	601
GREYFRIARS TREASURE, THE	(1910)	105
GREYFRIARS TREEE DWELLINGS, THE	(1918)	557
GREYFRIARS TRIPPERS, THE	(1914)	332
GREYFRIARS TYRANT, THE	(1911)	171
GREYFRIARS VENTRILOQUIST, THE	(1908)	32
HAND OF FATE, THE	(1923)	805
HAND OF AN ENEMY, THE	(1926)	938
HAND OF AN ENEMY, THE	(1927)	1001
HAND OF THE ENEMY, THE	(1923)	798
HAND OF THE MANDARIN, THE	(1930)	1179
HARD UP	(1914)	346
HARRY'S SACRIFICE	(1908)	12
HARRY WHARTON & CO. AFLOAT	(1909)	84
HARRY WHARTON & CO. IN AFRICA	(1922)	770
HARRY WHARTON & CO. IN EGYPT	(1932)	1279
HARRY WHARTON & CO. IN HOLLYWOOD	(1929)	1098
HARRY WHARTON & CO. IN INDIA	(1926)	965
HARRY WHARTON & CO. IN NEW YORK	(1929)	1094
HARRY WHARTON & CO. IN TEXAS	(1938)	1575
HARRY WHARTON & CO.'S BANK HOLIDAY	(1912)	234
HARRY WHARTON & CO.'S HOLIDAY	(1914)	340
HARRY WHARTON & CO.'S PANTOMIME	(1915)	409
GREYFRIARS VERSUS ST. JIM'S	(1908)	39
GREYFRIARS VICTORY, THE	(1908)	43
GREYFRIARS VISITORS, THE	(1909)	85
GREYFRIARS WHEELERS, THE	(1911)	166
GRUNTER OF GREYHURST	(1939)	1652
GUILTY GOLD	(1939)	1623
GUNPLAY AT GREYFRIARS	(1936)	1472
GUYED ON THE FIFTH	(1935)	1447
HARRY WHARTON & CO.'S RESCUE	(1913)	260
HARRY WHARTON & CO.'S WINDFALL	(1912)	218
HARRY WHARTON DECLARES WAR	(1932)	1287
HARRY WHARTON'S AMAZING REBELLION	(1936)	1498

Title	Year	No.
HARRY WHARTON'S BANK HOLIDAY	(1909)	78
HARRY WHARTON'S CAMPAIGN	(1909)	50
HARRY WHARTON'S CENTURY	(1910)	131
HARRY WHARTON'S CHRISTMAS NUMBER	(1913)	306
HARRY WHARTON'S CHRISTMAS GUEST	(1938)	1609
HARRY WHARTON'S DAY OUT	(1908)	42
HARRY WHARTON'S DIPLOMACY	(1914)	324
HARRY WHARTON'S DOUBLE	(1935)	1422
HARRY WHARTON'S DOWNFALL	(1911)	170
HARRY WHARTON'S DOWNFALL	(1925)	885
HARRY WHARTON'S DOWNFALL	(1932)	1257
HARRY WHARTON'S ELEVEN	(1909)	79
HARRY WHARTON'S ENEMY	(1928)	1063
HARRY WHARTON'S ENEMY	(1932)	1261
HARRY WHARTON'S ENEMY	(1935)	1424
HARRY WHARTON'S FEUD	(1926)	951
HARRY WHARTON'S LAST CHANCE	(1925)	888
HARRY WHARTON'S PERIL	(1910)	126
HARRY WHARTON'S PERIL	(1929)	1104
HARRY WHARTON'S 'PRO'	(1910)	138
HARRY WHARTON'S RECRUITS	(1909)	56
HARRY WHARTON'S RIVALS	(1917)	477
HARRY WHARTON'S SACRIFICE	(1921)	679
HARRY WHARTON'S SCHEME	(1908)	35
HARRY WHARTON'S SECRET	(1939)	1622
HARRY WHARTON'S TASK	(1908)	31
HARRY WHARTON'S TRIUMPH	(1935)	1427
HARRY WHARTON'S TRUST	(1920)	672
HARRY WHARTON'S WARD	(1909)	67
HARRY WHARTON'S WIN	(1912)	255
HARRY WHARTON WINS THROUGH	(1935)	1433
HAUNTED CAMP, THE	(1923)	800
HAUNTED CIRCUS, THE	(1936)	1485
HAUNTED ISLAND, THE	(1910)	149
HAZELDINE'S HONOUR	(1916)	412
HEAD OF STUDY 14, THE	(1910)	143
HEAD OF THE POLL	(1917)	481
HEAD'S HOLIDAY, THE	(1909)	82
HEART OF A HERO, THE	(1923)	813
HEAVY HAND, THE	(1937)	1521
HELD UP BY BANDITS	(1929)	1096
HE LET THE SIDE DOWN	(1938)	1604
HERALD'S RIVAL, THE	(1919)	612
HER BROTHER'S HONOUR	(1920)	648
HERLOCK SHOLMES OF GREYFRIARS, THE	(1917)	473
HERO OF GREYFRIARS, THE	(1909)	52
HERO OF GREYFRIARS, THE	(1916)	431
HERO OF THE CIRCUS, THE	(1936)	1489
HERO OF THE FIFTH, THE	(1928)	1058
HERO OF THE HOUR, THE	(1935)	1425

HEROES OF HIGHCLIFFE	(1915)	380
HEROES OF THE AIR	(1926)	980
HERO OF HOLLYWOOD, THE	(1929)	1100
HERO'S HOMECOMING, THE	(1919)	600
HER SCHOOLBOY CHUM	(1920)	662
HIDDEN FOE, THE	(1926)	940
HIDDEN HAND, THE	(1930)	1169
HIDDEN HORROR, THE	(1912)	239
HIDDEN PLUNDER	(1932)	1272
HIGH HAND, THE	(1934)	1391
HIGH JINKS AT HIGH OAKS	(1928)	1046
HIKER'S PRISONER, THE	(1933)	1338
HIS BLUNDERING BEST	(1921)	676
HIS BROTHER'S BURDEN	(1925)	925
HIS CONVICT COUSIN	(1936)	1493
HIS COUNTRY'S CALL	(1918)	560
HIS EXCELLENCY, COUNT BUNTER	(1922)	741
HIS FATHER'S HONOUR	(1917)	484
HIS FATHER'S SON	(1918)	537
HIS GUNMAN GUARDIAN	(1936)	1471
HIS HIGHNESS	(1916)	422
HIS LAST CARD	(1920)	664
HIS LAST MATCH	(1911)	197
HIS MAJESTY THE MAJOR	(1919)	588
HIS OWN BETRAYER	(1913)	279
HIS OWN FAULT	(1916)	443
HIS PAST AGAINST HIM	(1933)	1301
HIS RECORD CONDEMNED HIM	(1936)	1469
HIS SCAPEGRACE BROTHER	(1936)	1497
HOAXING OF HACKER, THE	(1939)	1617
HOLDING THE FORT	(1913)	277
HOLDING THE FORT	(1937)	1513
HOLD-UP AT GREYFRIARS, THE	(1920)	630
HOLD-UP AT GREYFRIARS, THE	(1930)	1163
HOME FOR THE HOLIDAYS	(1909)	47
HONOUR BEFORE ALL	(1912)	221
HONOURS EVEN	(1935)	1414
HOODED MAN, THE	(1940)	1664
HORACE COKER'S DARK DEED	(1936)	1473
HOSKIN'S CHANCE	(1919)	580
HOUSEBOAT MYSTERY, THE	(1921)	698
HOUSE OF DARK SECRETS, THE	(1939)	1640
HOUSE OF MYSTERY, THE	(1935)	1454
HOUSE OF PENGARTH, THE	(1923)	811
HOUSE OF PERIL, THE	(1937)	1542
HOUSE OF TERROR, THE	(1929)	1122
HOUSE ON THE HEATH, THE	(1916)	461
HOW LEVISON MINOR CAME TO GREYFRIARS	(1923)	793
HUN HUNTERS, THE	(1915)	372
HUNTED DOWN	(1927)	1009

Title	Year	No.
HUNTED DOWN	(1928)	1089
HUNTED DOWN	(1934)	1402
HUNTED HIKERS, THE	(1933)	1334
HUNTED MASTER, THE	(1932)	1253
HUNTED SCHOOLBOY, THE	(1933)	1307
HUNTING BUNTER	(1922)	738
HUNTING FOR TREASURE	(1918)	523
HUNTING FOR TROUBLE	(1932)	1291
HURREE SINGH'S PERIL	(1915)	379
HURREE SINGH'S SECRET	(1917)	496
HURREE SINGH'S SURPRISE PACKET	(1919)	611
IMPOSSIBLE FOUR, THE	(1913)	271
IMPOSSIBLE SCHOOLING, THE	(1931)	1223
IN ANOTHER'S NAME	(1913)	282
IN ANOTHER'S PLACE	(1918)	517
IN BORROWED PLUMES	(1913)	304
IN BORROWED PLUMES	(1920)	656
IN BORROWED PLUMES	(1922)	751
IN BORROWED PLUMES	(1928)	1066
IN DIREST PERIL	(1913)	278
IN HIDING	(1908)	8
IN HOT WATER	(1917)	466
INKY MINOR	(1911)	183
INKY'S PERIL	(1924)	845
IN MERCILESS HANDS	(1928)	1053
IN OPEN REVOLT	(1934)	1377
IN PERILOUS SEAS	(1926)	964
IN SPITE OF HIMSELF	(1918)	563
INTERLOPER, THE	(1927)	997
IN THE HEART OF THE HIMALAYAS	(1926)	967
IN THE POWER OF THE SHEIK	(1924)	868
INVASION OF GREYFRIARS, THE	(1909)	68
INVASION OF GREYFRIARS, THE	(1920)	641
INVISIBLE SCHOOLBOY, THE	(1937)	1538
IRON HAND AT GREYFRIARS, THE	(1924)	851
ISHMAEL OF THE FORM, THE	(1926)	976
ISLAND MYSTERY,AN	(1923)	816
ISLAND RAIDERS, THE	(1921)	712
ISLAND SCHOOLBOYS, THE	(1934)	1378
JAP OF GREYFRIARS, THE	(1922)	778
JAPE AGAINCT THE FIFTH, THE	(1912)	213
JAPE OF THE SEASON, THE	(1915)	407
JAPE OF THE TERM, THE	(1920)	626
JAPER OF GREYFRIARS, THE	(1926)	960
JAPER OF GREYFRIARS, THE	(1928)	1078
JAPER OF GREYFRIARS, THE	(1940)	1668
JESTER OF GREYFRIARS, THE	(1923)	791
JIMMY THE FOX	(1935)	1419
JIMMY THE ONE	(1932)	1252
JOHN BULL JUNIOR	(1911)	152

Title	Year	No.
LOOKING FOR ALONZO	(1914)	352
LORD BUNTER'S BODYGUARD	(1938)	1559
LOST IN THE CONGO	(1922)	771
LOYAL SIR JIMMY	(1918)	524
LOYAL TO THE LAST	(1927)	989
LUCK OF THE GIPSY, THE	(1923)	822
LURE OF THE GOLDEN SCARAB	(1932)	1280
MAD MUSICIANS AT GREYFRIARS, THE	(1933)	1304
MAILED FIST AT GREYFRIARS, THE	(1916)	424
MAKING OF HARRY WHARTON, THE	(1908)	1
MAN BEHIND THE SCENES, THE	(1938)	1597
MANDARIN'S VENGEANCE, THE	(1930)	1183
MAN FROM AMERICA, THE	(1920)	666
MAN FROM GERMANY, THE	(1940)	1680
MAN FROM SCOTLAND YARD, THE	(1930)	1148
MAN FROM THE CONGO, THE	(1922)	768
MAN FROM THE SEA,THE	(1937)	1507
MAN FROM THE SOMME, THE	(1918)	536
MAN FROM THE SOUTH SEAS, THE	(1927)	1017
MAN FROM THE STATES, THE	(1931)	1207
MAN IN THE MASK, THE	(1935)	1438
MAN IN THE MASK, THE	(1939)	1660
MAN OF MYSTERY, THE	(1939)	1662
MAN TRACKER OF UGANDA, THE	(1931)	1232
MAN WHO CAME BACK, THE	(1924)	854
MAN WITH THE GLARING EYES, THE	(1937)	1517
MAN WITH THE HIDDEN FACE, THE	(1938)	1580
MARK LINLEY'S LAST FIGHT	(1912)	252
MARK LINLEY'S TRIAL	(1921)	719
MAROONED	(1921)	686
MASKED TERROR, THE	(1929)	1108
MASTER WHO STAYED AT HOME, THE	(1915)	391
MATCH WITH ST. JIM'S, THE	(1914)	338
Mauleverer means business	(1923)	807
MAULEVERER'S DETECTIVE	(1916)	457
MAULEVERER'S PERIL	(1921)	692
MAULEVERER'S MISSION	(1920)	632
MAULY AND THE CARAVANERS	(1921)	706
MAULY'S AMAZING ADVENTURE	(1924)	835
MAULY'S FLIRTATION	(1915)	386
MAULY'S PALS	(1922)	755
MENACE FROM THE EAST, THE	(1937)	1543
MENACE OF TANG WANG, THE	(1930)	1175
MESSAGE FROM THE SEA, A	(1923)	790
MICK THE OUTCAST	(1923)	819
MICKY THE SPRAT	(1933)	1331
MICK THE UNTAMEABLE	(1923)	821
MICKY DESMOND'S LUCK	(1916)	425
MIDNIGHT MARAUDERS, THE	(1915)	402
MILLIONAIRE DETECTIVE, THE	(1933)	1330

Title	Year	No.
MILLIONAIRE STOWAWAY, THE	(1936)	1468
MISCHIEF-MAKER OF THE REMOVE, THE	(1935)	1405
MISSING CHINEE, THE	(1914)	318
MISSING FROM SCHOOL	(1919)	587
MISSING FROM SCHOOL	(1926)	982
MISSING MASTER, THE	(1914)	331
MISSING MASTERPIECE, THE	(1918)	558
MISSING SKIPPER, THE	(1917)	512
MONSIEUR WIBLEY	(1916)	438
MONTAGUE THE MYSTERIOUS	(1923)	814
MONTY NEWLAND'S ENEMY	(1929)	1127
MOONLIGHT FOOTBALLERS, THE	(1913)	293
MR BUNTER - FORM MASTER	(1922)	731
MUTINY	(1928)	1047
MUTINY ON THE FIREFLY	(1937)	1509
MYSTERIOUS FOE, THE	(1922)	756
MYSTERIOUS MR. MOBBS, THE	(1915)	389
MYSTERIOUS NIGHT RAIDER, THE	(1938)	1607
MYSTERY MAN OF EASTCLIFFE LODGE,THE	(1940)	1677
MYSTERY MAN OF GREYFRIARS, THE	(1939)	1616
MYSTERY MASTER, THE	(1930)	1145
MYSTERY MOONSTONE, THE	(1930)	1158
MYSTERY OF BLACKROCK ISLAND, THE	(1939)	1627
MYSTERY OF BUNTER COURT, THE	(1925)	913
MYSTERY OF CAVANDALE ABBEY, THE	(1930)	1192
MYSTERY OF GREYFRIARS, THE	(1908)	3
MYSTERY OF MARK LINLEY, THE	(1929)	1116
MYSTERY OF MR. QUELCH, THE	(1919)	610
MYSTERY OF MR. QUELCH, THE	(1938)	1603
MYSTERY OF MAULY, THE	(1916)	451
MYSTERY OF MOSSOO, THE	(1925)	894
MYSTERY OF NO. 1 STUDY, THE	(1932)	1271
MYSTERY OF POPPER'S ISLAND, THE	(1926)	953
MYSTERY OF PORTERCLIFF HALL, THE	(1935)	1435
MYSTERY OF VERNON-SMITH, THE	(1939)	1631
MYSTERY OF WHARTON LODGE, THE	(1928)	1038
MYSTERY OF WHARTON LODGE, THE	(1933)	1349
MYSTERY OF WHARTON LODGE, THE	(1938)	1610
MYSTERY OF THE GRANGE, THE	(1929)	1124
MYSTERY OF THE GREEN SATCHEL	(1932)	1275
MYSTERY OF THE HEAD'S HAT, THE	(1934)	1360
MYSTERY OF THE HEAD'S STUDY, THE	(1926)	942
MYSTERY OF THE METHUSELAH, THE	(1929)	1121
MYSTERY OF THE MILL, THE	(1931)	1208
MYSTERY OF THE PAPER CHASE, THE	(1931)	1197
MYSTERY OF THE POPLARS, THE	(1930)	1165
MYSTERY OF THE SILVER BOX, THE	(1970)	1157
MYSTERY OF THE CHRISTMAS CANDLES, THE	(1921)	723
MYSTERY OF THE GABLES, THE	(1915)	388
MYSTERY OF THE SILVER SCUD, THE	(1922)	758

MYSTERY OF THE VAULTS, THE	(1934)	1354
MYSTERY OF THE WARNING, THE	(1922)	733
MYSTERY ON THE THAMES	(1939)	1648
MYSTERY WRECK, THE	(1924)	872
MYSTIC CIRCLE, THE	(1915)	377
MY LORD BUNTER	(1937)	1556
MY LORD FISH	(1914)	337
NABOB'S DIAMOND, THE	(1908)	9
NABOB'S DOUBLE, THE	(1926)	961
NABOB'S RIVAL, THE	(1926)	969
NAP OF THE REMOVE	(1930)	1152
NAPOLEON OF GREYFRIARS	(1918)	540
NATIONAL SERVICE AT GREYFRIARS	(1917)	482
NAZI SPY'S SECRET, THE	(1940)	1682
NEW BOY AT GREYFRIARS, THE	(1908)	36
NEW BOY'S ENEMY	(1928)	1052
NEW BOY'S FEUD, THE	(1929)	1128
NEW BOY'S SECRET, THE	(1923)	779
NEW BOY'S SECRET, THE	(1926)	952
NEW FIRM, THE	(1910)	141
NEW PAGE, THE	(1911)	165
NEW SIXTHFORMER, THE	(1909)	49
NEW TERM AT GREYFRIARS, THE	(1909)	48
NIGHT RAIDERS, THE	(1931)	1224
NOBODY'S CHUM	(1926)	978

NOBODY'S PAL	(1932)	1293
NO-SURRENDER SCHOOLBOYS, THE	(1934)	1379
NO-SURRENDER SCHOOLBOYS, THE	(1937)	1512
NOT WANTED AT GREYFRIARS	(1936)	1470
NOT WANTED IN THE CIRCUS	(1936)	1487
NUGENT MINOR	(1910)	100
NUT OF GREYFRIARS, THE	(1913)	289
OLD BOY AT GREYFRIARS, AN	(1917)	510
OLD BOY'S CHALLENGE, THE	(1915)	385
OLD BOY'S VENGEANCE, THE	(1939)	1620
ONLY ALONZO	(1910)	137
ON THE IVORY TRAIL	(1922)	773
ON THE MAKE	(1917)	499
ON THE TEXAS TRAIL	(1938)	1574
ON THE TRAIL OF THE TRICKSTER	(1937)	1530
ON THE TRAIL OF TREASURE	(1935)	1439
ON THE WRONG TRACK	(1917)	495
ONE AGAINST THE SCHOOL	(1927)	1008
ONLY WAY, THE	(1911)	186
ORDER OF THE BOOT, THE	(1928)	1075
ORDERED TO QUIT	(1936)	1475
OTHER BUNTER, THE	(1916)	439
OUTCAST OF THE REMOVE, THE	(1924)	850
OUTCAST OF THE SCHOOL, THE	(1937)	1549
OUTLAW OF KALVA, THE	(1938)	1590

OUTSIDER, THE	(1935)	1458	PHANTOM OF THE ABBEY, THE	(1930)	1193
OUTLAWS OF THE SCHOOL, THE	(1911)	190	PHANTOM OF THE CAVE, THE	(1928)	1087
OUT OF BOUNDS	(1912)	225	PHANTOM OF THE HIGHLANDS, THE	(1923)	829
OUT OF BOUNDS	(1929)	1113	PHANTOM OF THE MOAT HOUSE, THE	(1939)	1661
OUTWARD BOUND	(1926)	963	PHANTOM OF PORTERCLIFFE, THE	(1935)	1436
PARTED PALS	(1917)	497	PHOTO PRIZE, THE	(1914)	351
PARTING OF THE WAYS, THE	(1912)	204	PHYLLIS HOWELL'S BROTHER	(1920)	628
PARTING OF THE WAYS, THE	(1924)	858	PLAYING THE GAME	(1928)	1064
PATRIOTIC SCHOOLMASTER, THE	(1914)	359	PLAYING THE GOAT	(1925)	899
PAYING THE PRICE	(1927)	1000	PLOT AGAINST THE SCHOOL, THE	(1921)	716
PEDRILLO OF GREYFRIARS	(1926)	946	PLOT THAT FAILED, THE	(1939)	1642
PENFOLD CUTS LOOSE	(1921)	720	PLOTTER, THE	(1939)	1641
PENFOLD THE BLADE	(1921)	721	PLUNDERED SCHOOL, THE	(1924)	844
PEN'S PAL	(1924)	843	PONSONBY PULLS THE STRINGS	(1937)	1519
'PEP' FOR THE 'FRIARS	(1925)	901	PONSONBY'S PAL	(1917)	507
PERFECT ALIBI, THE	(1939)	1633	PONSONBY'S PLOT	(1915)	393
PERIL FROM THE EAST, THE	(1930)	1176	PONSONBY'S REVENGE	(1922)	777
PERIL IN THE AIR	(1934)	1389	PONSONBY'S VICTIM	(1921)	673
PERIL OF THE NIGHT, THE	(1926)	962	POOR OLD BUNTER	(1911)	160
PERSECUTION OF BILLY BUNTER,THE	(1926)	956	POOR OLD BUNTER	(1925)	896
PERSECUTION OF MR. PROUT, THE	(1922)	763	POP OF THE CIRCUS	(1930)	1166
PETER THE PLOTTER	(1924)	852	POPPER COURT TEA PARTY, THE	(1936)	1480
PETER TODD'S CHANCE	(1913)	275	POPPER'S UNPOPULAR PRIZE	(1933)	1309
PETER TODD'S PLOT	(1914)	314	POSTAL ORDER CONSPIRACY, THE	(1910)	133
PETER TODD'S VENGEANCE	(1917)	486	PREFECTS AT WAR	(1929)	1112

REMOVE DETECTIVES, THE	(1939)	1657
REMOVE EIGHT, THE	(1910)	122
REMOVE ELECTION CAMPAIGN, THE	(1917)	480
REMOVE ELEVEN ON TOUR, THE	(1915)	405
REMOVE EXAM MYSTERY, THE	(1921)	713
REMOVE FORM'S FEUD, THE	(1912)	229
REMOVE MASTER'S SUBSTITUTE, THE	(1908)	28
REMOVE RUGGER TEAM, THE	(1922)	730
REMOVE TO THE RESCUE, THE	(1910)	109
REMOVE'S CHALLENGE, THE	(1910)	118
REMOVE'S REMARKABLE RECRUIT, THE	(1935)	1409
REMOVE'S RECRUIT, THE	(1920)	647
REMOVE'S RECRUIT, THE	(1935)	1460
RETURN OF THE NATIVE, THE	(1919)	585
RETURN OF THE PRODIGAL, THE	(1914)	357
RETURN OF THE REBELS, THE	(1928)	1049
RIGHT SORT, THE	(1914)	310
RIGHTING A WRONG	(1926)	948
RIGHT THING, THE	(1919)	615
RISE AND FALL OF WILLIAM GOSLING, THE	(1919)	617
RIVAL CO'S OF GREYFRIARS, THE	(1912)	215
RIVAL ENTERTAINERS, THE	(1908)	41
RIVAL OARSMEN	(1925)	918
RIVAL SCHOOLS, THE	(1908)	34
RIVAL SCOUTS	(1909)	65
RIVAL TREASURE SEEKERS, THE	(1927)	1024
RIVAL TUCKSHOPS, THE	(1925)	904
RIVAL VENTRILOQUIST, THE	(1915)	361
RIVAL WEEKLY, THE	(1911)	159
RIVALS AND CHUMS	(1923)	792
RIVALS FOR A FORTUNE	(1934)	1373
RIVALS FOR RICHES	(1938)	1563
RIVALS OF GREYFRIARS, THE	(1909)	61
RIVALS OF GREYFRIARS, THE	(1916)	459
RIVALS OF THE CHASE	(1917)	506
RIVALS OF THE REMOVE	(1908)	7
RIVALS OF THE REMOVE	(1935)	1423
RIVALS OF THE RIVER	(1921)	685
RIVALS' TEST, THE	(1912)	212
ROAD TO RUIN, THE	(1912)	224
ROGER OF THE REMOVE	(1927)	994
ROGUE IN THE REMOVE, A	(1929)	1130
ROGUE'S REMORSE, THE	(1931)	1202
ROLLING DOWN TO RIO	(1936)	1462
ROLLING IN DOLLARS	(1930)	1161
ROLLING IN MONEY	(1911)	154
ROUGHING IT	(1908)	18
ROUGH ON COKER	(1914)	327
ROUGH ON HIS RIVAL	(1939)	1635
ROUGH ON REDWING	(1918)	555

Title	Year	No.
RUCTIONS AT HIGHCLIFFE	(1914)	344
RUCTIONS IN ROME	(1934)	1388
RUCTIONS IN THE REMOVE	(1914)	308
RUCTIONS ON THE RANCH	(1938)	1577
RUCTIONS ON THE RIVER	(1939)	1644
RUNAWAY, THE	(1914)	323
RUNAWAY, THE	(1938)	1601
RUNAWAY REBEL, THE	(1932)	1296
RUNAWAY SCHOOLBOY, THE	(1937)	1553
RUNAWAY'S RETURN, THE	(1921)	674
RUN OUT OF GREYFRIARS	(1939)	1656
RUN TO EARTH	(1916)	437
SACKED !	(1918)	565
SACKED FROM THE SCHOOL	(1912)	250
SAMUEL AND SAMMY	(1918)	567
SANDOW GIRL OF GREYFRIARS, THE	(1913)	283
SAVED FROM DISGRACE	(1911)	181
SAVED FROM SHAME	(1918)	534
SAVED BY A FOE	(1938)	1598
SAVED BY HIS ENEMY	(1935)	1445
SAVED BY HIS ENEMY	(1938)	1605
SAVED FROM THE CANNIBALS	(1931)	1236
SAVED FROM THE SACK	(1935)	1432
SAVED FROM THE SEA	(1930)	1186
SAVED FROM THE SEA	(1933)	1314
SAVED BY A SCAPEGRACE	(1932)	1295
SAVING A SCAPEGRACE	(1934)	1370
SAVING BUNTER'S BACON	(1939)	1614
SAVING HIS ENEMY	(1932)	1266
SAVING THE BOUNDER	(1917)	511
SCAPEGOAT, THE	(1913)	303
SCAPEGRACE OF THE SCHOOL, THE	(1932)	1292
SCAPEGRACE OF THE THIRD, THE	(1925)	924
SCARING THE SCHOOL	(1921)	678
SCHEMER OF THE REMOVE, THE	(1928)	1062
SCHEMER OF THE REMOVE, THE	(1935)	1408
SCHEMER OF THE REMOVE, THE	(1938)	1566
SCHEMER OF THE SIXTH	(1932)	1288
SCHEMERS OF STUDY NO. 7	(1936)	1492
SCHOLARSHIP COMPANY, THE	(1920)	640
SCHOOLBOY ACROBATS, THE	(1915)	378
SCHOOLBOY ARTIST, THE	(1920)	653
SCHOOLBOY AUCTIONEER, THE	(1915)	365
SCHOOLBOY BARBER, THE	(1919)	607
SCHOOLBOY BROADCASTERS, THE	(1927)	991
SCHOOLBOY CONJURER, THE	(1913)	268
SCHOOLBOY CINEMA STARS, THE	(1920)	660
SCHOOLBOY CRACKSMAN, THE	(1931)	1213
SCHOOLBOY CRUSOES, THE	(1938)	1591
SCHOOLBOY DETECTIVE, THE	(1912)	230

Title	Year	No.
SCOURGE OF THE RED DRAGON, THE	(1930)	1181
SCOUT'S VICTORY, THE	(1915)	384
SCUTTLED SCHOONER, THE	(1938)	1593
SECOND FORM MYSTERY, THE	(1918)	549
SECRET OF SHARK'S TOOTH, THE	(1924)	847
SECRET OF THE CARAVAN, THE	(1921)	705
SECRET OF THE CAVES, THE	(1923)	812
SECRET OF THE DUGOUT, THE	(1940)	1669
SECRET OF THE HOLIDAY ANNUAL, THE	(1933)	1340
SECRET OF THE OAK, THE	(1931)	1225
SECRET OF THE OLD OAK, THE	(1934)	1380
SECRET OF THE PRIORY, THE	(1932)	1268
SECRET OF THE SCARAB, THE	(1932)	1283
SECRET OF THE SCHOONER, THE	(1928)	1077
SECRET OF THE SEA CAVE, THE	(1939)	1629
SECRET OF THE SMUGGLERS CAVE, THE	(1936)	1499
SECRET OF THE TURRET, THE	(1931)	1246
SECRET OF THE VAULTS, THE	(1934)	1393
SECRET OF THE WATER LILY, THE	(1939)	1650
SECRET OF THE WIRES, THE	(1919)	608
SECRET SEVEN, THE	(1934)	1394
SECRET SNIPER, THE	(1931)	1194
SELF-CONDEMNED	(1914)	339
SENT TO COVENTRY	(1911)	189
SENT TO COVENTRY	(1927)	1033
SENTENCE OF THE SCHOOL, THE	(1916)	447
SENTENCED BY THE FORM	(1924)	859
SEXTON BLAKE MINOR	(1939)	1618
SHADOW OF SHAME, THE	(1920)	663
SHADOW OF THE SACK, THE	(1936)	1496
SHADOW OF THE SACK, THE	(1940)	1683
SHADOWED BILLIONAIRE, THE	(1934)	1386
SHADOWED IN SOUTH AMERICA	(1936)	1464
SHADOWED MILLIONAIRE, THE	(1937)	1523
SHADOWED SCHOOLBOY, THE	(1932)	1282
SHADOWED SCHOOLBOY, THE	(1934)	1367
SHADOW OF THE PAST, THE	(1914)	334
SHADOW OF THE UNDERWORLD, THE	(1931)	1214
SHARING THE RISK	(1917)	492
SHIELDING A SCAPEGRACE	(1916)	418
SHIP OF SECRETS, THE	(1937)	1508
SHIPWRECKED SCHOOLBOYS, THE	(1909)	62
SHUNNED BY THE FORM	(1913)	288
SHUNNED BY THE FORM	(1928)	1083
SHYLOCK OF GREYFRIARS, THE	(1929)	1110
SHYLOCK OF GREYFRIARS, THE	(1933)	1327
SHYLOCK OF THE SECOND, THE	(1918)	545
SIGNOR'S SECRET, THE	(1936)	1488
SILENT STRIKE, THE	(1920)	631
SINISTER DOCTOR SIN, THE	(1937)	1541

Title	Year	No.
SON'S DILEMMA, A	(1920)	671
SOUTHERN SEAS, THE	(1927)	1021
SOUTH SEA ADVENTURERS	(1938)	1589
SOUTHWARD BOUND	(1932)	1278
SPECIAL CONSTABLE COKER	(1915)	375
SPECTRE OF HOAD CASTLE, THE	(1933)	1335
SPECTRE OF POLPELLY, THE	(1935)	1453
SPEEDWAY COKER	(1931)	1220
SPIRITED AWAY	(1914)	345
SPLIT IN THE CO., A	(1923)	808
SPLIT IN THE SIXTH, A	(1913)	262
SPLIT IN THE STUDY, A	(1916)	446
SPOOFING ALONZO	(1911)	155
SPOOFING THE SCHOOL	(1912)	235
SPOOFING THE SCHOOL	(1937)	1536
SPORTING CHAMPION, THE	(1923)	786
SPORTS DAY AT GREYFRIARS	(1919)	606
SPORTS DENIAL WEEK AT GREYFRIARS	(1913)	287
SPORTSMAN OF THE FOURTH, THE	(1939)	1613
SPORTSMEN ALL	(1915)	390
SPORTSMEN FROM THE NORTH	(1921)	696
SPORTS OF THE SCHOOL, THE	(1913)	286
SPORTS WEEK AT GREYFRIARS	(1925)	903
SPOTTING THE SECRET	(1939)	1612
SPRING'S BROTHER	(1918)	564
SPY OF THE SIXTH, THE	(1936)	1495
SPYING FORM MASTER, THE	(1934)	1368
SPY OF THE GESTAPO, THE	(1940)	1681
SPY OF THE FIFTH, THE	(1935)	1441
SPY OF THE SIXTH, THE	(1932)	1294
SQUIFF'S SECRET	(1920)	629
STAGE STRUCK	(1908)	16
STANDING BY SKINNER	(1913)	274
STANDING BY SMITHY	(1935)	1431
STANDING BY SNOOP	(1919)	578
STANDING BY THEIR PALS	(1924)	853
STAR OF THE CIRCUS, A	(1926)	945
STAUNCH CHUMS	(1909)	89
STAY-IN STRIKE AT GREYFRIARS, THE	(1937)	1511
STICKING TO HIS GUNS	(1916)	442
STOLEN CUP, THE	(1911)	198
STOLEN DIARY, THE	(1922)	746
STOLEN GUY, THE	(1921)	717
STOLEN SCHOOLBOYS, THE	(1912)	231
STOLEN STUDY, THE	(1916)	452
STONY BROKE	(1909)	66
STRAIGHT AS A DIE	(1915)	403
STRAIGHT AS A DIE	(1923)	783
STUDY ON TOUR	(1910)	123
SUNDAY CRUSADERS, THE	(1915)	400

Title	Year	No.
VENGEANCE OF THE WOLF, THE	(1936)	1465
VENGEANCE OF WOO FING, THE	(1921)	694
VENTRILOQUIST AT LARGE, A	(1927)	1030
VENTRILOQUIST'S PUPILS, THE	(1909)	57
VENTRILOQUIST'S VENGEANCE, A	(1938)	1567
VERNON SMITH'S FEUD	(1924)	860
VERNON SMITH'S LAST FLING	(1940)	1673
VERNON SMITH'S RETURN	(1920)	624
VERNON SMITH'S VICTORY	(1920)	625
VERY GALLANT GENTLEMAN, A	(1918)	520
VICTIMS AND VICTORS	(1916)	464
VICTORY	(1917)	505
VICTORY FOR THE REBELS	(1930)	1174
VISCOUNT BUNTER	(1917)	474
VOICE OF THE TEMPTER, THE	(1931)	1200
WAGGIE OF THE REMOVE	(1919)	591
WAKING UP ALONZO	(1921)	687
WAKING UP GREYFRIARS	(1930)	1167
WALKER OF THE SIXTH	(1918)	562
WALKER ON THE WARPATH	(1938)	1584
WALLY BUNTER'S LUCK	(1919)	569
WALLY OF THE REMOVE	(1919)	571
WALLY'S WHEEZE	(1919)	579
WALLY WINS THROUGH	(1922)	735
WANDERER'S RETURN, THE	(1939)	1658
WANTED BY THE POLICE	(1930)	1144
WAY OF THE REBEL, THE	(1932)	1289
WAY OF THE TRANSGRESSOR, THE	(1916)	462
WAY OF THE TRANSGRESSOR, THE	(1936)	1504
WAY OF THE WIZARD, THE	(1931)	1218
WAYWARDNESS OF WIBLEY, THE	(1924)	832
WHARTON & CO. VERSUS MERRY & CO.	(1909)	64
WHARTON'S OPERATIC COMPANY	(1908)	15
WHEN FRIENDS FALL OUT	(1916)	423
WHEN JOHNNY COMES MARCHING HOME	(1915)	376
WHEN ROGUES FALL OUT	(1919)	577
WHEN THE HEAD RESIGNED	(1922)	743
WHILE GREYFRIARS SLEPT	(1932)	1254
WHIP HAND, THE	(1918)	519
WHIP HAND, THE	(1925)	927
WHIP HAND, THE	(1927)	1022
WHITE FEATHER, THE	(1914)	316
WHITE FEATHER, THE	(1924)	837
WHITE SLAVES OF THE CONGO	(1931)	1234
WHO HACKED HACKER ?	(1930)	1156
WHO PUNCHED PROUT ?	(1928)	1085
WHO PUNCHED PROUT ?	(1930)	1188
WHO SACKED HACKER ?	(1939)	1621
WHO SHALL BE CAPTAIN ?	(1935)	1426
WHO WALLOPED WIGGINS ?	(1932)	1276

THE MAGNET

Controlling Editors

1908 - 1911 Percy Griffith (pres. dec'd)

1911 - 1916 Herbert Allan Hinton

1916 - 1919 John Nix Pentelow (d.1931)

1919 - 1940 Charles Maurice Down

by Quidnunc

In one sense the Magnet was the brainchild of an Amalgamated Press Editor, Percy Griffith, who thereupon became this new paper's first editor, too. In another sense it might be said that if it truly had any human father that man was Charles Hamilton who, as a direct result of its birth, was going to be better known for the rest of his life as Frank Richards.

If magazines had to have birth certificates the precise parentage of this one might be long debated. But, in the end, it is likely that the exact truth would be stated, incomplete as it is, and that in the appropriate place on the form would be written succinctly 'Magnet, son of Gem'.

Percy Griffith had launched this other, earlier paper on March 16th 1907 with only the vaguest of ideas of what its grown shape would actually be, and as is the case with so many children the toddling, tottering infant didn't much resemble the eventual man. It carried adventure stories from a prolixity of pens alternately with fortnightly school stories from one 'Martin Clifford'. In brief, it had a confused childhood, but it grew up fast.

Eleven months later the adventure stories, as such, were gone for good, and Griffith knew precisely what sort of a paper the Gem would be for the rest of its life : a good paper and a school-story paper. And he knew more. Readers were clamouring for another paper like it. Not one identical with it, but one evolved from it.

Son of Gem, thy name is Magnet : an irresistible and enduring force of attraction. Who can deny sixty-six long years later that the name was most apt? And so, on February 15th 1908, the Magnet was born.

MYSTERY

Percy Griffith, the man, the first editor, remains much of a mystery. We are not certain of the date or the place of his death; we don't even know when, or where, he was born. Hardly anyone now alive remembers him, and the few people who do are most reluctant to talk. All that anyone can, or will, say is that he was a bohemian type and a great talker; lively, quick-witted and energetic.

The reader could probably glean all that is known of him from Frank Richards' Autobiography, particularly when armed with the knowledge that Griffith was the 'V.C.' Richards also referred to.

Griffith was assisted in the Magnet and Gem office by Herbert Allan Hinton, his second-in-command, and by a sub-editor, Charles Maurice Down. The office boy was R.T. Eves, who in later years founded the School Friend, and eventually joined the Board of Amalgamated Press as a director.

Meantime, in 1911, Percy Griffith suddenly, and hurriedly, left Fleetway House for an unknown overseas destination, and that was the last anyone saw of him. It is now presumed that he is long dead. Nicknamed 'Pushful Percy' for his ability to get things done and squeeze the utmost out of his authors there is little doubt that his wild streak of bohemian improvidence, touched on by Richards in his Autobiography, ruined what would otherwise have been a most remarkable career in the realm of boys' fiction.

Certainly much credit is due to him for creating the most famous boys' paper in history.

CONTRAST

Following Griffith's dramatic exit, his second-in-command Herbert Allan Hinton took over: a man whose temperament contrasted completely with that of his predecessor in every respect. Born in 1880, Hinton had been educated at a public school, and was distantly related to Alfred Harmsworth, the founder of The Amalgamated Press. Nicknamed 'Trooper' because of his connection with the Kent Yeomanry, he was a man of magnificent physique and much addited to black cigars. This despite his moralistic preaching on the evils of smoking in his companion paper The Boys' Friend.

Frank Richards always claimed that George Figgins of St. Jim's was modelled on Hinton, but this has been disputed. According to a sub-editor who knew him well, the character who bore most resemblance to Hinton was Larry Lascelles, the games master at Greyfriars.

***

1914 came, and the beginning of the first world war, and almost immediately the Companion Papers' staff in Fleetway House was decimated as, one after another in rapid succession, sub-editors 'answered their Country's call' and volunteered for war service. C.M. Down – by this time chief sub-editor - was the first to go. He took a commission in August 1914, and was closely followed by Hedley O'Mant, Noel Wood-Smith, W.E. Stanton Hope, W.E. Pike, G.R. Samways and H.W. Twyman, who was later to become editor of the Union Jack.

Surprisingly, H.A. Hinton did not go until 1916, when he joined the Coldstream Guards with the rank of Captain. Meanwhile, in his editorials, he made great play of receiving flocks of white feathers from readers, all intimating that he was a coward. Coward he was certainly not; astute editor he equally certainly was. The white feathers were wholly imaginary, conjured up to inject some controversy into his columns, and at the same time to do something towards linking the fiction of Greyfriars with the cold, cruel outside world of implacable fact.

CRICKET

After 1916, its office denuded of staff, a writer was hurriedly called in to steer the paper through the rest of the war, and the man appointed was probably the most controversial editor of all. John Nix Pentelow, this third editor of the Magnet, was born at St. Ives, Huntingdon, in 1872, his father being the local grocer. He had begun writing at an early age, having his first story published when he was only fifteen, and he had rapidly become both versatile and prolific. School stories, sports stories and adventure stories all flowed from his pen.

Fiction apart, he was an acknowledged authority on cricket and the author of several books on the game as well as being a regular contributor to Wisden. He also, for a time, co-edited 'Cricket' with A.C. MacLaren, the famous Test Captain, and was a member of the Middlesex, Sussex, and Surrey Cricket Clubs.

Although only forty-four years of age when he became editor of the Magnet and the Gem in 1916, he looked at least twenty years older. Business worries had prematurely aged him, and his hair was white, his shoulders bowed. He was also very deaf and as he scorned the use of a hearing aid a quiet conversation with him usually ended up jarring the windows throughout Fleetway House.

He was also much given to switching topics in the middle of a discussion, a stroke of one-upmanship only the very deaf can successfully play, and many a prickly printer or carping contributor with an unanswerable grievance to air suddenly found himself as a consequence, and much to his chagrin, up to his vigorously vibrating ear-drums in a very one-sided, mind-bending dialogue about the merits and demerits of W.G. Grace.

For all that he was a kindly man, and many writers of repute today speak highly of the help he gave them in their early years. Probably the greatest criticism aimed at his editorship was that he himself wrote a disproportionate number of the Greyfriars and St. Jim's stories published during the last two years of the war, though it is difficult to see what else he could have done with no material coming from Charles Hamilton, and nearly all the substitute writers away on active service.

KILLING OFF COURTNEY

A further criticism which has been levelled strongly over the years and shows no signs of ever abating concerns the fact that he 'killed-off' Arthur Courtney, the Greyfriars sixth-former, in Magnet number 520 – entitled 'A Very Gallant Gentleman'. Many Magnet readers consider this to be unforgiveable, though in fairness to Pentelow it must be recorded that it was revealed recently that he only did so on instructions from higher authority. It seems there was evidence that readers were confusing Courtney with Frank Courtenay – but this one Captain of the Highcliffe Fourth, and as a result the order went out that one of them had to go.

Pentelow did, however, add a character of his own creation to the Greyfriars Remove in the person of Piet Delarey, the boy from South Africa. But Delarey dropped out of the stories soon after Pentelow's editorship ended in 1919.

To Pentelow's eternal credit were his painstaking and careful studies of the history and characters of Greyfriars and St. Jim's which appeared in his Galleries, and these have been acclaimed by even his severest critics. Further, and this achievement can never be belittled, he kept the papers going through very difficult years indeed.

NEW YEAR TRAGEDY

With the end of the war and the return of the former staff, Herbert Allan Hinton resumed the editorship of the Companion Papers, and John Nix Pentelow moved on to become editor of the Boys' Realm and Sport and Adventure, together with several smaller libraries. Eventually retiring from the staff of the Amalgamated Press in 1923, Pentelow died at Carshalton in Surrey in 1931, at the age of fity-nine.

Meantime, Hinton's second occupancy of the editor's chair did not last for long. Like Percy Griffith before him he had acquired somewhat expensive tastes, and in 1921 he was caught out in the plagiarism of a Greyfriars story, which led him to leave Fleetway House somewhat abruptly. Thereafter he founded his own boys' paper, entitled School and Sport, and at the outbreak of the second world war was editing Dalton's Weekly.

Six years later, whilst in a train near Weybridge Station on New Years' Day, 1945, during the blackout, Hinton opened the door of the carriage furthest away from the platform and fell to his death. He was widely mourned. Despite his failings he was a jovial, friendly man, and one whom one could not help liking.

LISPLESS GUSSY

The fourth, and last, editor of the Magnet was Charles Maurice Down, a tall, distinguished, military-looking man, and one who had been on the staff of the Companion Papers from the very first issues of the Gem and the Magnet. He was, as a result, quite the most experienced editor the paper ever had, and also quite easily the most successful.

Son of a Justice-of-the-Peace, he had had a public school education, and was a gentleman in every sense of the word.

Charles Hamilton made no secret of the fact that he based one of his most universally popular characters on him, that of D'Arcy – better known as 'Gussy' – the Swell of St. Jim's, and for anyone who has ever had the privilege of meeting him it is easy to see why. Though it should be stated that Mr. Down does not speak with a lisp!

Probably his greatest single contribution to the Greyfriars saga was made when he conceived the idea of producing the Holiday Annual, which was not only the most popular annual of all in its time, but remains easily the one most sought-after by collectors today – evidence the fact that copies change hands at considerably more than the original price.

COKER ASCENDING

Whilst the favourite Greyfriars character of other editors is not known, Mr. Down thought Horace James Coker of the Fifth easily the best, and much more credible than Billy Bunter, whom he did not really care for. Certrainly there were some classic stories of Coker in his period of office, and it was his opinion that, if persevered with, Coker could well have become as famous as the fat Owl of the Remove.

During his twenty years as controlling editor of the Companion Papers – which now included many others beside Magnet and Gem, such as Modern Boy and the famous Schoolboys' Own Library – and with the assistance of sub-editors Hedley O'Mant, Noel Wood-Smith (both now deceased), R.C. Hewitt and Arthur Aldcroft, all – as Frank Richards put it – was calm and bright. Richards himself undoubtedly wrote his best stories during this period, and from 1932 onwards the editor never had to worry again about finding a substitute story, for the flow of manuscripts from Charles Hamilton never ceased.

In May 1940 the last Magnet appeared on the bookstalls and Charles Maurice Down put all his records and papers together with the manuscripts of unpublished stories and other material into large boxes and deposited them in a director's office, from whence – no-one knows how, when, or why – they duly disappeared.

Perhaps they contributed in some way to the war effort; perhaps they were simply destroyed; perhaps one day, they will turn up again, as suddenly and as inexplicably as when they vanished thirty long years ago. Truth is frequently stranger than fiction, as the fascinating story of the Magnet itself certainly shows.

As for Charles Maurice Down, in semi-retirement he first served the Army and Navy Stores as a consultant, and then later went into his own family business. Now completely retired in Hertfordshire he must often look back – as he has earned the right to look back, and with pride – to the part that he played, and it was a big one, in helping to produce throughout its whole life the most popular school-story paper of all time.